Job and Income Security for Unemployed Workers

SOME NEW DIRECTIONS

Saul J. Blaustein

The W.E. Upjohn Institute for Employment Research

Library of Congress Cataloging in Publication Data

Blaustein, Saul J., 1924-
    Job and income security for unemployed workers.

    1. Manpower policy—United States. 2. Insurance,
Unemployment—United States. 3. Economic security—
United States. 4. Job security—United States.
5. Unemployed—United States. I. Title.
HD5724.B553   362.8'5   81-10423
ISBN 0-911558-83-7   AACR2
ISBN 0-911558-84-5 (pbk.)

THE INSTITUTE, a nonprofit research organization, was established
on July 1, 1945. It is an activity of the W. E. Upjohn Unemployment
Trustee Corporation, which was formed in 1932 to administer a fund
set aside by the late Dr. W. E. Upjohn for the purpose of carrying on
"research into the causes and effects of unemployment and measures
for the alleviation of unemployment."

THE AUTHOR

Saul J. Blaustein, a graduate in 1948 of The City College of New York, studied graduate economics in subsequent years at the University of California in Los Angeles and at George Washington University. He was employed in the U.S. Department of Labor from 1951 to 1967, at first with the Bureau of Labor Statistics where he worked on price index and cost-of-living research. In 1955 he joined the staff of the Unemployment Insurance Service of the Labor Department's former Bureau of Employment Security where he specialized in unemployment insurance research and in program policy development and evaluation.

Mr. Blaustein came to the Upjohn Institute in 1967. He developed and directed the Institute's series of 16 studies in unemployment insurance and chaired the Unemployment Insurance Research Advisory Committee as part of that effort. More recently, he worked closely with the National Commission on Unemployment Compensation. He has written many articles and monographs on unemployment insurance and related fields, and has consulted and lectured extensively in these areas.

iv

FOREWORD

Long-standing public programs, many dating back to the 1930s, are coming under increasing strain and scrutiny. Those dealing with the problems of unemployed workers are prominent among them. Minor modifications and additions may not be enough to achieve the extent of reform needed to make existing programs viable in our contemporary setting. Saul Blaustein's proposed regrouping of unemployment insurance and related programs designed to deal with the needs of unemployed workers represents the reasoned type of reform worth considering.

The W.E. Upjohn Institute is pleased to publish this monograph by one of its staff researchers not only because of the fresh approach it describes, but also because it addresses a continuing and persistent dilemma of our times—the waste of human resources resulting from unemployment. In drawing together diverse programs of income support and employment services around the central goal of reemployment, the proposed scheme restores a focus that has become at least partially neglected over the years. The suggested restructuring of our present unemployment insurance program and establishment of a new unemployment assistance program represent major departures from current approaches, and the strong emphasis on reemployment efforts makes the whole scheme responsive to the growing sentiment that the problem often calls for more than income support. Mr. Blaustein's long experience in research and analysis of unemployment insurance and related matters lends authority to his ideas and makes them deserving of serious consideration.

v

Facts and observations presented in this monograph are the sole responsibility of the author, and do not necessarily represent positions of the W.E. Upjohn Institute for Employment Research.

E. Earl Wright
Director

Kalamazoo, Michigan
June 1981

PREFACE

Many of the ideas assembled in this monograph draw upon thinking and discussion extending back over a period of 25 years involving numerous colleagues and others in the fields of unemployment insurance, employment and training, and welfare. The initial opportunity to bring these ideas together within the concept of a new integrated system came in 1976 when the Michigan Department of Labor's Bureau of Employment and Training requested some alternative approaches for the state's unemployment insurance program. The result was a report made in 1977 entitled *A New Job Security System for Michigan.*

The preface to that earlier report set forth the following as the guiding point of view:

> A fundamental consideration in developing program alternatives has been to place unemployment insurance in a total context of government policy and action for helping the unemployed. In giving effect to that orientation, a major assumption is made that the basic focus of whatever assistance that is supplied to the unemployed must be on moving them into productive employment and a position of self support. It was important, therefore, to consider carefully the total context and suggest how it could more effectively center on that assumption.

That same thought applies equally in the present monograph.

In the reformulation, the Job Security System is placed in a national orientation thereby overcoming a number of dilemmas when viewed on a state basis only. The System and its principal components receive further and fuller development as well. The intent is to stimulate debate and other new ways of thinking about the continuing problems of unemployment and the means for dealing with them.

Of the many individuals who encouraged me and commented very helpfully on this work, I feel moved to single out a few who perhaps can stand for all who did so. These include Ralph Altman, Father Joseph M. Becker, Jerry Beideman, Philip Booth, Raymond Munts, William Papier, George F. Rohrlich, and David W. Stevens. I am also grateful to Wilbur J. Cohen who invited me to present some of these ideas, particularly with respect to unemployment insurance, to the National Commission on Unemployment Compensation. That presentation yielded further useful comments and was summarized as "A Proposal for a New Job Security System With Three Tiers of Unemployment Insurance" in Volume 1 of *Unemployment Compensation Studies and Research* accompanying the Commission's *Final Report,* July 1980.

Finally, I must acknowledge the diligence and patience of the supporting staff at the Upjohn Institute in seeing the monograph through many drafts to its final form. Any remaining shortcomings are my responsibility alone.

CONTENTS

I. INTRODUCTION

"I'm mighty glad to get this check, but getting back on the job is even better."

—Niels R. Ruud

"We have started to pay unemployment benefits in Wisconsin. . . . but let's not forget that steady work and wages will always be better than unemployment benefits."

—Paul Raushenbush

These two statements were made July 1, 1936 in Madison, Wisconsin on the occasion of the first unemployment insurance benefit payment ever made in the United States.[1] In his terse remark, the recipient expressed perfectly the appropriate perspective about the benefit payment. The response by Mr. Raushenbush, the first and long-time director of the Wisconsin program and one of the "fathers" of unemployment insurance in this country, underscored the joint objectives of income support and reemployment. In both statements, the emphasis on the latter is clear.

This monograph describes a new framework, called the Job Security System,[2] which would integrate the various

---

1. *American Labor Legislation Review,* September 1936, p. 102.

2. This title is used to distinguish the proposed system from the present federal-state system made up of state employment security agencies operating unemployment insurance and employment service programs.

1

public programs designed to help experienced unemployed workers find work and to alleviate their unemployment. The scheme's main purpose is to organize these programs systematically and cohesively and focus them on the goal of employment. Its core objective is getting unemployed workers into suitable jobs. No one served by the proposed system is outside the labor force; each is capable of working and available for work. The presumption is that everyone who applies for help in finding work or for income maintenance during unemployment wants a job and is seeking one.

By and large, clients of the Job Security System are unemployed workers with established labor force attachment. New entrants and reentrants to the labor force may also be served, but they are likely to be aided more directly by programs provided under the Comprehensive Employment and Training Act (CETA), especially if there is a problem of low income and a lack of skills or work experience. The CETA programs are outside the proposed system. The Job Security System and CETA programs, however, must coordinate their services to assure that no one seeking employment who can be helped is neglected.

Besides job search assistance and other employment services, the Job Security System (JSS) provides income support consisting, for the most part, of two types of wage-loss compensation: unemployment insurance (UI) and a new program of unemployment assistance (UA). UI is available as a matter of right to covered unemployed workers who meet certain employment-related conditions, such as past and current labor force attachment. UA would be available to the noninsured unemployed—those who exhaust UI benefits or are not covered by UI—who meet similar conditions plus an income test. In addition, the system would administer a number of special programs that supplement UI for certain categories of unemployed workers, such as trade adjustment assistance for workers adversely affected by foreign imports. The system may also pay cash benefits or allowances in connection with specific adjustment activities, such as retraining and relocation, when undertaken by unemployed workers.

The JSS deals with the unemployed as individuals and with individual employers who want workers. It does not, as such, treat the general problem of unemployment, of general insufficiency in the demand for labor. That is the concern of fiscal, monetary, and other economic policies. The proposed system's main thrust is to guide the unemployed labor supply to the jobs available and, to the extent it can, to help bring about the most efficient employment of the labor supply. In the process, the system would constantly update and improve its knowledge of the labor market to identify jobs which are available and employers who are likely to need workers.

The expectation is that nearly all unemployed workers assisted by the system will become reemployed within a reasonable period of time, most within a few months. It must be emphasized, however, that this expectation can be realized only if the economy is in good health and generates a strong demand for labor. If labor demand is weak, the number of jobless workers will increase, as will the average duration of their unemployment, and the system will be less successful in achieving its goal despite its best efforts on behalf of clients. The value and effectiveness of the JSS will be most evident when there are jobs to be filled.

Justification for the New System

Many public programs now exist for aiding the unemployed. They include the state employment or job services and various CETA programs operated by local government units and by states. These programs offer job search and related employment services, vocational training, other vocational adjustment services, and temporary public service employment.[3] Other public programs provide various forms of income support for the unemployed. These include unemployment insurance, welfare payments through the federally subsidized Aid to Families with Dependent Children (AFDC)-Unemployed Father program,[4] disaster unemployment assistance, a growing number of special programs aimed at compensating workers for job loss resulting from certain government policies,[5] and limited local or state general assistance that may be available for needy persons, including some who are unemployed.[6] Some federal programs provide other forms of financial assistance for the unemployed, such as food stamps, Medicaid, and housing subsidies; these are also available to persons who are not in the labor force. Some of the unemployed who are in public training programs may receive training allowances.[7]

These programs began and evolved over the past 50 years, many of them within the last 20 years. Since problems of the unemployed are varied and numerous, it is not surprising that the measures devised to help overcome these problems are also varied and numerous. Taken together, the public programs available represent an extensive set of policies

3. At the time of writing (early 1981), the public service employment programs under CETA are being curtailed and scheduled to terminate by October 1981.

4. The standard AFDC program may also be included in this listing since some adult recipients must register for work with the public employment service and be available for work. Not all AFDC recipients, however, are required to do so, such as those caring for small children or for family members who are sick or disabled.

5. These include, among others, Trade Adjustment Assistance (as provided under the Trade Act of 1974), the Redwood Employee Protection Program, two Railroad Employee Protection Programs, Urban Mass Transportation Protection, and the Airline Employee Protection Program.

6. The railroad UI program is not part of the present federal-state system and remains outside the proposed new system. Ideally, and eventually, it too should be included.

7. Other public income maintenance programs, such as social security-old age insurance, also supply support for the unemployed although that is not their particular objective. See Merrill G. Murray, *Income for the Unemployed: The Variety and Fragmentation of Programs,* (Kalamazoo, MI: The W.E. Upjohn Institute for Employment Research, April 1971), p. 70.

ministering to the needs of unemployed persons. It is fair to ask, then, what the proposed new system can add. Why is it desirable to establish another or a different approach in an area already addressed by so many approaches? What does the proposed system offer that is different and significantly better than what present arrangements provide?

The Job Security System is designed not so much as a new *additional* approach for aiding the unemployed, but rather as a means for pulling existing programs together into a more coherent, integrated, and coordinated set of activities. Many of the existing programs developed at different times to meet specific needs without taking sufficient account of other programs already in place which served similar purposes. A new program may have emerged because an existing program did not serve a particular need adequately or as precisely as desired, and because it often was easier to create a separate approach than try to adapt or improve a larger established program. There has been, for example, a proliferation of special programs (see footnote 5) aimed at specific industries or groups of workers who are dislocated because of a public policy, such as tariff reduction agreements with other countries, or deregulation of a particular industry. These programs single out limited groups of workers for special treatment usually more generous than that provided by the more general programs.[8]

Another kind of development has been the partial redirection of an existing program to serve purposes it was not originally intended or designed to serve. The use of unemployment insurance, for example, to compensate for very long term unemployment during 1975-1977 (up to 65 weeks in some cases) went far beyond that program's

8. For a description and discussion of these programs, see Mamoru Ishikawa, *Unemployment Insurance and Proliferation of Other Income Protection Programs for Experienced Workers,* Unemployment Insurance Occasional Paper 80-1 (Washington, DC: U.S. Department of Labor, Employment and Training Administration, Unemployment Insurance Service, 1980).

original conception. The increased refocusing of the AFDC program on availability for work or training for many of its adult recipients is another example of a significant change in direction that places strains on a program's conceptual base and structure.

The motivations for these new developments have usually been quite reasonable and sound, and the approaches taken may also have been reasonable and sound up to a point. As new developments accumulate over time, however, without adequate coordination, confusions and inefficiencies multiply. Both duplications and gaps in services and support for the unemployed may develop. There may be unequal treatment of the unemployed without justification that is apparent to recipients. Administrative responsibilities are fragmented. Programs may conflict or work at cross purposes, and tendencies develop to lose sight of intended goals. Administrative difficulties increase and funds may be wasted. Both those who pay for the costs of these services and those who receive them have reason to complain. When such conditions accumulate to major proportions, it is time to consider consolidation and reform. The Job Security System is proposed as a means for such consolidation and reform.

The new system would also provide an opportunity to establish a common and consistent conceptual base for these programs, and that may be its most important justification. Too often, programs have narrow objectives and fail to take account of broader or more primary goals. More adequate income support for unemployed workers is an important purpose sought by some of the new special programs, but overconcentration on that objective can diminish emphasis on assisting the process of reemployment. To a large extent, the failure to pursue the latter goal more vigorously is a problem of administrative priorities and inadequate financing rather than statutory intent. The UI program has always required claimants to be available for work and to seek work, and looks to the employment service (ES) to assure their exposure to jobs. The ES, however, is continually diverted to place higher priorities on serving groups other than UI claimants, thereby reducing the reemployment emphasis for the latter. Moreover, the ES staff nationally has remained fixed in size for 15 years despite its heavier responsibilities, which effectively bars any significant improvements in its services. The proposed JSS builds emphasis on the reemployment objective directly into its procedures so that it cannot be neglected so easily.

To repeat the point made at the outset, it is the premise of the new system that suitable reemployment is its core objective. Income support is a vital factor, but it should not overshadow the ultimate goal of employment; it should be administered so as to support that goal as well as to alleviate hardship. The fact, for example, that recipients of AFDC or of state and local general assistance include both labor force participants and nonparticipants makes those programs ill-suited to pursue the employment objective for the former. The Job Security System alters the income support arrangements for labor force participants now under these programs to correct for that deficiency.

Failure to pursue the employment objective vigorously has contributed to general public criticism of income maintenance programs. Much of the public regards these programs as too generous and too easily available to too many individuals who are suspected of being unavailable for work or unwilling to work, despite what they claim openly. Whether or not such criticism is fully justified, the lack of emphasis on reemployment assistance helps to convey and sustain the impression held. The proposed system offers the opportunity to reestablish the primacy of employment and thereby respond to public concerns over income maintenance programs.

Another supporting argument for the proposed system is that it may open the way to resolve some problems in several existing programs that appear to have become intractable. By incorporating these existing programs within the system and integrating them around the central orientation of employment assistance, some restructuring and improvements can be made which may resolve their problems more readily than possible within their current contexts.

The public employment services, for example, require revitalization and strengthening. Their active integration with UI and other income assistance within the JSS stresses the reemployment goal for recipients and restores the employment service to the major role contemplated for it earlier but which has become increasingly remote over the years. Employment service financing requires reform and expansion which may have a better chance under the JSS design.

The federal-state UI program currently faces serious problems which appear very difficult to resolve within its present structure, at least in a way that would attract broad agreement. Under the proposed JSS, the UI program would be restructured to emphasize close integration with reemployment assistance. The new structure also offers a way of treating two major problems that bedevil the present program—the duration of UI protection and financial insolvency.

The establishment of a new unemployment assistance program within the proposed new system seeks to rationalize the treatment of some AFDC recipients as labor force participants and to close the gaps that exist in the support of other needy unemployed persons. Welfare reform proposals continue to mix welfare and employment assistance without adequate distinctions among recipients so that the latter can be applied effectively. The incorporation of UA within the

JSS would make that distinction clear. Welfare reform could then deal more readily with those AFDC recipients who cannot work or are not expected to work.

General Design

The JSS proposal calls for a comprehensive and integrated system that provides various employment assistance services and income support to unemployed workers, and to some underemployed workers as well. The system combines, restructures, and improves upon present employment and income support programs to assure closer coordination among them, greater efficiency of their operations, and more complete coverage of the needs of the unemployed. It assumes that private sector activity and public economic policies will keep overall unemployment levels within manageable bounds; the system's services and support are likely to prove inadequate and ineffective under conditions of prolonged mass unemployment no matter how well organized and integrated they are.[9]

At all times, the Job Security System emphasizes employment promotion efforts to help jobseekers find satisfactory work. Income support is viewed as a temporary measure available only when reasonable employment is not available and while jobseeking efforts proceed. Income support is important to the unemployed, but its provision must not obscure the focus on promotion of reemployment. If unemployment continues for a very long period, particularly under generally normal labor market conditions, the individual's employability may require reevaluation. The possibility must be considered that the very long term jobless worker may in fact be unemployable. That individual might

9. One hesitates to specify a particular limit above which unemployment would be considered unmanageable, but peak unemployment rates experienced in the 1975 recession period would surely qualify as such if continued for very long.

be offered a place in a sheltered workshop program or shifted to the Supplemental Security Income program currently available for the disabled and the aged who need such support.

While the proposed JSS is national in scope, it is designed to operate essentially through state-administered programs. State UI and job services would continue, but subject to some modifications or adaptations required by restructuring under the new system. Federal and state governments would continue as partners in the system, but the balance of responsibility and control would shift more towards a national orientation with regard to the problem of long term unemployment. The shift reflects a recognition that when unemployment becomes increasingly prolonged for individual workers, the means required to support them and to resolve their problems may lie increasingly beyond the capacities of local and state resources.

Central to the Job Security System is the registration of jobseekers for work and the listing of as many job openings as possible at the public employment or job security offices. The key is the establishment of a genuine, fully-functioning labor exchange. With some exceptions, registration would be compulsory for all those seeking income support and employment assistance provided under the system.

Jobseekers would be diagnosed and classified according to their need for job search assistance. Assistance could range from simply providing access to a listing of job openings to planning and facilitating substantial training or rehabilitation. Where a job is not immediately available, the unemployed worker may draw income support if eligible. Following initial diagnosis, the system would provide for further review, at appropriate times, of the registrant's job search activities and reassessment of need for help if unemployment continues. The advice and assistance supplied would then change accordingly.

Since most subsidized public service employment and training for the unemployed are now organized and administered through decentralized CETA programs, the Job Security System must coordinate its activities closely with these programs. How best to achieve the proper coordination between CETA and the public employment service is currently an uncertain and controversial matter. No attempt is made here to deal with the question. Evaluation of CETA-employment service relations should be pressed to illuminate the problems. Their resolution should aim at serving the best interests of jobseekers and employers. Through improved collection and analysis of labor market information, the JSS would continuously monitor the need for employability development services, training, and public service employment for its clients. Such information and analysis also form an important base for planning CETA programs. Because eligibility rules exclude many unemployed workers from CETA programs, the JSS should have the flexibility of providing similar types of services to such workers when the need is indicated.

Income support supplied through the Job Security System is identified clearly as support for labor force participants. Income support for nonparticipants should be supplied outside this system. Some of the present welfare programs mix the two. These should be redesigned so that labor force participants now serviced through welfare programs would receive their support through the JSS. A major innovation proposed with JSS is the establishment of a new unemployment assistance program to supply income support to needy unemployed jobseekers who are not eligible to receive unemployment insurance. Unemployment assistance would replace present welfare support for those who are able to work and expected to seek employment and who have some work experience. Like unemployment insurance, UA would be available as a weekly benefit.

Under the proposed system, unemployment insurance is restructured as a three-tiered program to cover short, medium, and long term unemployment, and to limit its total scope to the first 39 weeks of unemployment. The full extent of UI protection would be available to eligible unemployed workers at all times; the payment of long term benefits would not depend on the rate of unemployment. Any support beyond the UI limit would be supplied through the unemployment assistance program. The new arrangement eliminates special extensions of unemployment benefits during recession periods. Each UI tier has its own eligibility requirements and job search conditions. The proposed method of financing UI benefit costs is geared to the three-tiered arrangement.

The Job Security System, as proposed, also encompasses other forms of support and employment assistance, such as training allowance supplements, relocation assistance, and other rehabilitation measures.

The proposed system takes account of the varied composition of the unemployed as analyzed in terms of certain characteristics that are relevant to distinguishing job search service and income support needs. In describing the plan, this monograph proceeds first with an analysis of the system's potential clientele in terms of some of these characteristics. It then discusses the types of services and income support provided under the system for each clientele category. The type of services and support available, and the manner in which they are supplied, may vary at different stages of an individual's unemployment or with the condition of the relevant labor market. These distinctions are important and also noted. Following this presentation of what the system offers for different categories of the unemployed, each type of proposed service or income support is more fully described with regard to content and financing, with particular emphasis on explaining changes from existing arrangements, the reasons for the changes, and some opposing arguments.

Recently, the National Commission on Unemployment Compensation (NCUC) completed a two and one-half year study of the federal-state UI program and related problems.[10] Many of the concerns of the Commission overlap those addressed by the JSS proposal. Where appropriate, NCUC recommendations will be indicated and discussed in this monograph.

10. *Unemployment Compensation: Final Report,* National Commission on Unemployment Compensation, Washington, DC, July 1980.

II. POTENTIAL CLIENTELE
OF THE JOB SECURITY SYSTEM

Table 1 analyzes the unemployed labor force by sex-age categories and by reasons for unemployment. The latter concern whether or not the unemployed had been working just prior to their unemployment and, among those who had, the nature of their job separation. Data are shown for 1975 and 1979 to compare a recession year with a year of lower unemployment. Not only is the total level of unemployment different between the two years, but the distributions by reasons for unemployment are also different. In 1975, for example, workers on layoff and job losers together comprised over half (55 percent) of the unemployed compared with 43 percent in 1979. These unemployed workers account for most of the insured unemployed; in 1975 and 1979, insured unemployment made up about 63 and 44 percent, respectively, of all unemployment.[1]

The data in the table represent annual average levels of unemployment for each year. The total number of persons experiencing unemployment at any time during the year is much larger. It was 21.1 million in 1975 and 17.9 million in 1979.[2] Information available about all persons experiencing unemployment during the year does not permit their analysis by reasons for unemployment. Their numbers, however, af-

---

1. Based on data in *Economic Indicators,* March 1980, p. 13.

2. Data from *Employment and Training Report of the President,* 1980, p. 303, and from *News* from the Bureau of Labor Statistics, September 18, 1980.

Table 1
Potential Unemployed Clientele of Proposed Job Security System by Reason for Unemployment, Sex and Age Annual Averages, 1975 and 1979

Reason for unemployment	1975				1979			
		Age 20 and over		Age 16		Age 20 and over		Age 16
	Total	Male	Female	to 19	Total	Male	Female	to 19
All unemployed								
Thousands	7,830	3,428	2,649	1,752	5,963	2,223	2,213	1,528
Percent	100.0	100.0	100.0	100.0	100.0	100.0	100.0	100.0
Previously employed	65.8	83.5	63.9	34.3	57.1	77.7	53.6	32.3
On temporary layoff	21.2	28.8	20.5	7.6	14.0	20.8	13.1	5.4
Job losers	34.2	46.2	29.5	18.0	28.8	42.8	24.2	15.1
Job leavers	10.4	8.5	13.9	8.7	14.3	14.1	16.3	11.8
Not previously employed	34.2	16.5	36.1	65.7	42.9	22.3	46.3	67.6
Reentrants	23.8	14.5	31.9	29.9	29.5	19.3	40.0	29.0
New entrants	10.4	2.1	4.2	35.8	13.4	3.0	6.3	38.6

SOURCE: *Employment and Earnings*, January 1977, p. 147, and January 1980, p. 168.

ford some idea of the volume of potential clients of the Job Security System.[3]

Most of the unemployed were working just prior to their unemployment—66 percent in 1975 and 57 percent in 1979. Reentrants and new entrants into the labor force constitute the rest of the unemployed. Of this category, about four out of five were women or teenagers, in both years.

The following discussion elaborates further on the composition of each category of unemployed individuals, thereby providing some background in preparation for the later description of the services that would be supplied by the Job Security System.

Unemployed Workers—Previously Employed

These are workers who have temporarily or permanently separated from their jobs. They can be divided into three groups on the basis of the temporary or permanent nature of the separation and whether the permanent separation was voluntary or involuntary.

Workers on temporary layoff

This group consists of workers who are placed on temporary layoff with expectation of recall. They remain attached to their jobs though not on the active payroll. Certain job-connected fringe benefits may continue for these workers. The group subdivides further on the basis of the expected length of the layoff or the degree of assurance of recall, factors that are not always clear or definite. For various purposes, it is useful to distinguish between workers on a specific short term or limited term layoff, say for no more

3. Over 11 million workers began drawing UI benefits in 1975 and over 8 million in 1979 (from *Handbook of Unemployment Insurance Financial Data,* U.S. Department of Labor, Employment and Training Administration).

than 30, 60, or 90 days, and those on a longer or indefinite layoff. The indefinite layoff can turn out to be long term or permanent; at some point it is advisable for such an individual to pursue prospects for alternative employment. Most workers on short term layoffs do not actively seek other jobs.

About 55 to 60 percent of this group consist of adult men and about a third or more, adult women; the small remainder are teenagers. The proportion of the unemployed who are on temporary layoff is substantially higher during recession periods. Nearly all of them are eligible to draw UI benefits.

Job losers

These are workers who have been separated from their jobs involuntarily. They divide into the following three subgroups with varying implications for income support eligibility:

Workers discharged because of misconduct;
Workers retired compulsorily from their jobs;
All other involuntary job losers.

Regardless of the reason for job loss, unemployed workers in these subgroups are considered able to work, available for work, and in an active search for work. Workers fired for misconduct are disqualified from drawing UI, at least for a period of time.

Unemployed retirees may receive pensions, but they still want and seek work. Normally, they qualify for UI benefits. In some cases, the strength of their continued attachment to the labor force comes under question. The pension received may be deducted from their UI benefits, leaving reduced weekly benefits or none at all.[4]

---

4. A federal provision requires the states to deduct certain pensions drawn by claimants, including social security pensions, from their UI benefits.

Most other job losers are eligible to draw UI. Adult men make up about 55 to 60 percent of all job losers, adult women account for about 30 percent, and the rest are teenagers.

Job leavers

These workers have resigned or quit their jobs voluntarily. As unemployed, they are assumed to be available for and seeking work. They are not eligible to draw UI, at least for a period of time, unless they left for a good cause that is acceptable for UI purposes.

In some cases, the distinction between a job leaver and a job loser is not absolutely clear. The reason for the separation, or whether there was "good cause" for leaving, may be disputed between the worker and the former employer. On the one hand, the worker may feel that the employer exerted great pressures, subtle or not so subtle, to force a quit, in which case the separation was tantamount to a discharge. On the other hand, the worker may really want to leave but arranges to be fired, or induces the employer to do so, to avoid a voluntary-quit disqualification for UI benefits. The problem of making the appropriate distinction affects UI eligibility more than it does the administration of job services.

The proportion of the unemployed who are voluntary job leavers declines in recessions. It was about 10 percent in 1975 compared with 14 percent in 1979. In 1975 and 1979, over 35 percent of all job leavers were adult men and over 45 percent were adult women; the remainder, about 20 percent, were teenagers.

Unemployed Persons—Not Previously Employed

This category consists of people who have never worked before (new entrants) or who left the labor force for a time after the last job they held (reentrants). Reentrants are the more sizable group, over twice as numerous as new entrants.

Reentrants

This group reflects a wide range of circumstances, varying by how long the individual was out of the labor force; whether the last job was regular or temporary, intermittent, or part-time; and whether the reentrant currently seeks a regular permanent job or a temporary one.

Among reentrants in 1975 and 1979, about 45 and 50 percent, respectively, were adult women; the rest were split about evenly between adult men and teenagers.

One important distinction that should be made is between those who had some employment during the year preceding reentrance (or during a base period as defined for unemployment insurance purposes) and those who did not. Among reentrants who did work recently, those who lost their jobs before they left the labor force may be eligible for UI benefits when they return to seek work.

New entrants

Strictly speaking, this group represents people who never worked before; they are seeking their first jobs. Most are youths who are still in school, or who have just finished or left school. About 75 percent of all new entrants in both 1975 and 1979 were teenagers. Of the remainder, the majority were adult women.

It is useful to distinguish between new entrants seeking temporary or short term employment and others looking for regular jobs with expectations of long term labor force attachment. An individual who has worked before but only on temporary or short-time jobs for limited periods and who was not a regular labor force participant may at some point become interested in regular, permanent employment. While classified as a reentrant, that person is, in effect, a new entrant into the regular labor force.[5] The administration of job services must take account of these circumstances.

Underemployed Workers

While most clients of the Job Security System are likely to be totally unemployed persons, others who are currently employed may also apply and qualify for services. Some work part time but want full-time jobs. Others in full-time jobs may feel they are working below their abilities and skills and seek better jobs. Some in temporary or seasonal jobs which will soon end seek other employment before job separation occurs. These groups together comprise what may loosely be called the underemployed. Consistent with its goal of promoting the most economically efficient use of our labor resources, the JSS would provide assistance to these workers in finding full employment.

The number of underemployed workers who seek or want full-time or better jobs is difficult to pin down. Information exists about workers employed part time (less than 35 hours per week) from the monthly Current Population Survey, the source of much of our labor force statistics. In 1980, an average of nearly 23 million persons worked part time during the weeks surveyed.[6] About 10.7 million of them did not want or were unable to work at full-time jobs. Another 8.0 million worked less than 35 hours a week because of time lost due to illness, vacation, holidays, bad weather, and other noneconomic reasons, or because the job was normally scheduled for less than 35 hours a week. The remaining 4.2 million worked part time for economic reasons. Over half of

5. As defined by the Bureau of Labor Statistics, new entrants include persons who were previously employed only part time or who worked full time for less than 2 weeks.

6. Data from *Employment and Earnings,* January 1981, pp. 190-191.

these workers were on short-time due to "slack work," and most usually worked full time. Most who usually worked part time did so because they could only find part-time work. Of the nearly 4 million nonagricultural workers employed part time for economic reasons, 54 percent had jobs in the trade and service industries, 47 percent were less than 25 years old and 53 percent were female.

A survey conducted in May 1976 identified 3.3 million fully employed workers who were seeking other jobs for the following reasons:[7]

Higher wages or salaries . . . . 34 percent
Better hours or working conditions . . . . 11 percent
Better advancement opportunities . . . . 10 percent
Current job ending, including temporary
   or seasonal job . . . . 11 percent
Better use of skills . . . . 9 percent
Other reasons . . . . 25 percent

Some of these workers could also be classified as underemployed.

As potential clients of the JSS, underemployed workers do not include those who, as a matter of choice, work on a part-time or temporary basis or at levels below their capacities. Among involuntarily underemployed workers who might turn to the JSS for assistance, it is useful to determine whether their current underemployment is the result of a temporary reduction of the usual work schedule or a permanent characteristic of the job itself.

Workers on temporarily reduced work schedules

This group is similar in many respects to workers placed on temporary layoffs. The latter can be seen as an extreme

---

7. *Monthly Labor Review,* March 1977, p. 60.

case of a temporary cutback in the normal work schedule. Unless the cut in the workweek is especially deep, the present unemployment insurance programs in most states provide no compensation for lost wages even on a partial benefit basis. If the reduced work schedule is for a short period, the workers affected are not likely to be seeking other jobs or to require employment services. The proposed new structure for UI benefits would include improved partial benefit provisions that accommodate work sharing through reduced schedules.

In 1979, on average, there were over 1.4 million workers employed part time for economic reasons who usually worked full time; in recession year 1975, this group numbered 1.8 million.[8] Included were workers who lost full-time jobs and took temporary part-time jobs until they could find full-time work.

Workers seeking other employment

One component of this group consists of workers who expect their current jobs to terminate and who are able to seek other jobs beforehand. Included are workers on temporary or seasonal jobs and those already notified that their jobs will end in the near future. If possible, such workers should be looking for further employment to avoid or minimize any subsequent unemployment. It is, however, difficult and often impossible to do so while still working full time. Job search services for these workers could be beneficial, especially if available after working hours.

Other underemployed jobseekers working below their capabilities seek jobs that better fulfill their potentials. Job search assistance can serve an upgrading function for such workers. Some unemployed job leavers may have been

---

8. *Employment and Earnings,* January 1980, p. 184, and January 1976, p. 150.

motivated to quit because they were underemployed in this sense. To the extent they succeed in finding better employment, the jobs vacated may become available to unemployed workers with lesser capacities.

III. TREATMENT OF CLIENTELE CATEGORIES

This chapter describes how the proposed Job Security System functions with respect to the unemployed and underemployed as grouped by the foregoing classifications. Most of the unemployed will enter a local JSS office to file for UI benefits or unemployment assistance (UA), or to seek help in finding work, or both. How they are treated will depend on the reasons for their unemployment, how long unemployment has continued, and the current condition of the labor market. How and what kind of employment services are rendered will depend also on the individual's education, training, job experience, and occupational skills.

The stage of a workers' unemployment is an especially important consideration with regard to the job services and income support supplied, as well as to how they are administered. When the worker draws benefits, the conditions of eligibility and the type of benefits paid may change as unemployment becomes more and more prolonged. Generally speaking, major changes in these respects are assumed to occur at three-month intervals. This assumption underlies the proposed reorganization of the present federal-state UI program into the new three-tiered program.

While admittedly arbitrary, the three-tiered arrangement would force a deliberate reconsideration of the worker's circumstances and the need for any change in the job search approach being followed. If circumstances warranted, a review would be made even before the end of the three-month period. In the past, the UI program has applied the practice of periodic interviews of claimants, but not consistently or on a sustained basis. Often, determining the claimant's continuing eligibility for benefits has received much greater emphasis than determining the claimant's job search needs. Experiments in the late 1960s and early 1970s with individualized analysis and treatment of the reemployment needs of claimants encouraged further development of this approach, but budgetary constraints interfered. The current Eligibility Review Program has revived those efforts and is working toward widespread application in all states.[1] How well it succeeds depends heavily on resources allocated to the approach and on how far state agency officials are willing and able to push the idea down the line. So far, results appear mixed.

The formal move from one tier to the next under the restructured UI program would assure that a close review is made as needed, both for eligibility and job search purposes. It would impress the thought on both the claimant and the counselor that a new stage has begun which may call for some changes in attitude about the strategy and nature of the job search. Each tier would provide 13 weeks of benefits, but the eligibility conditions specified for each tier would be different and increasingly demanding. The tiers, successively, would compensate for short term, medium term, and long term unemployment. Beyond the third tier, income support would no longer be provided on an insurance basis, but would be available as unemployment assistance on the basis of an income text. Chapters V and VI describe in more detail these two income support programs under the proposed system.

---

1. The federal-state UI program is currently pursuing efforts to establish similar procedures for claimants through its Eligibility Review Program, outlined in General Administration Letter No. 5-77 issued to all state agencies on December 21, 1976 by the U.S. Department of Labor's Employment and Training Administration.

The general level of unemployment and local labor market conditions would also influence the way job services and income support are administered. Unlike the present UI program, the proposed system would not automatically extend UI when unemployment reaches specified levels. Labor market conditions, however, would affect the services and benefit eligibility requirements, and how they do so is generally covered in this discussion.

The key individuals of the JSS staff involved directly with the unemployed worker would be the job search counselor and the benefit reviewer. In dealing with the UI claimant, both would work closely together; they would be located in the same office. A similar team would work with UA claimants, though perhaps in a different part of the office so as to keep the two programs distinct.

The counselor must be knowledgeable about current labor market conditions and job search practices, and about how different occupations and skills relate to each other so as to identify a range of jobs that the claimant can reasonably consider seeking. The counselor must also be aware of the availability of specialized services, e.g., aptitude testing, retraining and rehabilitation, to which the claimant can be referred, if appropriate. The benefit reviewer would apply the eligibility requirements and see that the claimant understands them. Both the counselor and the reviewer together would diagnose and reassess the claimant's job prospects at the start of each UI tier and at other times as needed. They would also consult together and with the claimant in developing a job search plan. The benefit reviewer would monitor the claimant's job search to see how well the plan is followed or if it needs change. Emphasis is always on encouragement and assistance to the claimant in finding employment. The expectation underlying this emphasis is that the true attitudes of the claimant with regard to desire and availability for work are more readily revealed in the context of a positive approach than in a direct attempt at the outset to question the claimant's labor force attachment and behavior.

Unemployed Workers—Previously Employed

Workers on temporary layoff

All workers on a temporary layoff would be eligible for first-tier (short term) UI benefits, assuming they meet the minimum base-period employment and earnings qualifying requirements for this tier.

If recall to work is scheduled or definitely expected to take place within 30 days of the layoff, the worker would not need to register at the employment service or actively seek other employment during this period to maintain eligibility for benefits. The worker who wishes to do so may apply for job search services. If recall is expected after 30 days and within 90 days, the same conditions prevail. The worker's recall status, however, should be reconfirmed with the employer 30 days (or 4 weeks) and again 60 days (8 weeks) after the layoff.

If recall is not expected within 90 days, or if the layoff is or becomes indefinite, the worker must register for work and have a diagnosis made of reemployment prospects as a condition for receiving UI. The diagnosis normally would be made when the worker files for the fourth or fifth week of benefits. If the labor market involving the individual's type of work is clearly in a recession, the required diagnosis could be delayed for several more weeks. If the layoff continues beyond eight weeks and remains indefinite, a job search plan would be prepared and implemented. If local labor market conditions continue unfavorable, however, that step could be postponed until after tier 1 benefits are exhausted.

Workers on a temporary layoff who do not qualify for first tier UI because of insufficient past employment may be eligible for unemployment assistance, depending on household income. If job recall prospects are indefinite or likely to take more than 90 days to materialize, the same treatment applicable to UI claimants would apply to UA recipients as well.

Workers on layoff who exhaust their short term (tier 1) UI and continue to be unemployed would be treated the same as other job losers who exhaust tier 1.

Job losers—workers discharged for misconduct

Workers who qualify for tier 1 but have been discharged for misconduct would not be paid UI benefits for a period of weeks after which, if still unemployed, they could draw their benefits. At the end of the disqualification period, their job search experience and job prospects would be reviewed and any advisable adjustments in job search activity suggested. That review could occur earlier, during the disqualification period, at the claimant's request. These claimants should be urged to take advantage of other job services—testing, counseling, etc.—that may be appropriate in view of the circumstances of their discharge. In other respects, they would be treated in the same way as other job losers who draw UI. Discharged workers who do not qualify for UI on the basis of past employment but who do meet UA requirements may become eligible for UA following a disqualification period. They would receive similar review and advice regarding their job search.

Job losers—other involuntarily separated workers

Leaving aside for the moment older workers forced to retire from their jobs, all other job losers include those laid off permanently for reasons which do not give rise to benefit disqualification. These include separations made because of business declines or shutdowns; staff reductions by non-profit employers or government in response to budget cuts; worker dislocations resulting from technological or organizational changes, plant relocation, or other structural changes in industry; and discharges of employees because of unsatisfactory performance on the job. Some business declines may be temporary or seasonal, and workers laid off may have good prospects for rehire by their former employers even though not given a specific assurance of recall. An indistinct line separates such workers from those placed on a temporary but indefinite layoff.

Under the proposed system, all job losers in this category who can satisfy the minimum qualifying requirements would be entitled to tier 1 UI benefits, provided they also meet all the usual conditions of availability for work, registration with the employment service, regular reporting to file claims, and active search for work. At an early stage (within the first few weeks of filing), a brief diagnosis of reemployment pro-spects would be made to classify these workers into two groups: the job ready and the less readily employable jobseekers.

The job ready. These are workers who have viable skills and experience that are in demand in the local job market, and who have reasonable prospects of finding new suitable jobs in the next 8 to 10 weeks. In some cases, they may already have located jobs that will start during this period and therefore may be treated as workers on temporary, short term layoffs. Others should be urged to use any job search services or techniques that could be helpful, both within and outside the public employment office. If job search con-tinues for more than 8 to 10 weeks, the worker's job pro-spects should be reviewed and reevaluated. The worker may need more intensive job search help, particularly with regard to search methods, or some supportive counseling if there appear to be any personal impediments to the job search. As appropriate, the worker should be advised to consider whether job expectations are too high in the light of current labor market conditions. It may be too early to press for lower expectations if the worker is still considered "job ready," but the idea could be suggested at this stage. Refusal, without good cause, to take a suitable job that is offered or to follow up on a referal to such a job would be grounds for a disqualification from UI benefits. Evidence of unreasonable restriction on availability for work or inadequate pursuit of a job would also be grounds for benefit suspension.

A job-ready worker who exhausts tier 1 benefits could file and qualify for tier 2. Once beyond the short term range of the UI program, a more intensive review would be made of the worker's job prospects, job search, and other service needs. The worker's situation should be reassessed about every two months, and more frequently if warranted. A definite job search plan should be prepared and implemented, or an earlier plan reevaluated. Some lowering of job expectations may be urged at this time and pressed harder if the job search remains unsuccessful. The approach, however, should be positive and reasonable in the light of current conditions of the labor market; there must be no harassment of the claimant. If the job market outlook is temporarily bleak, the jobseeker could be encouraged to consider taking temporary, including part-time, work until prospects improve, if such employment is available and feasible. The claimant would not be *required* to take such employment while still drawing tier 2 benefits, but could be increasingly pressed to do so as time goes on.

If unemployment continues beyond the 26th week of benefits, the worker may file and qualify for tier 3 benefits, but the conditions would become more demanding. If the worker continues to be considered "job ready"—that is, his or her skills and experience are still viable in the labor market—the problem is probably one of a temporary but prolonged recession. At the time the claimant files for tier 3 benefits, job readiness should be reconfirmed. If not confirmed, the worker may then be a candidate for vocational adjustment service (training, etc.) and, in general, treated as a less readily employable jobseeker. If still job ready but a victim of recession, the worker can be referred to temporary jobs, including part-time work, if available, even if such employment falls outside the usual line of work and somewhat below the usual earnings experience. The jobs must be suitable and reasonable in other respects, however. They may include temporary public service jobs established during recession periods. Failure to accept such employment without good cause would disqualify the worker from further UI.

Job-ready unemployed workers who wish to explore possibilities for retraining or other adjustments through public programs should be given every consideration possible. If appropriate training and resources are available, they should have access to them as long as it is clear that they are unlikely to become reemployed during the period of the training and that the training would enhance future reemployment prospects. It may be reasonable for unemployed workers to utilize a period of unfavorable reemployment prospects to improve their job capacity through training. Such efforts toward upgrading should be encouraged and supported. While in training, workers may be eligible to receive training allowances to supplement their UI or UA benefits.

The less employable jobseeker. These job losers are either structurally unemployed workers whose skills or experience are no longer in demand in the local labor market, or marginal workers with few or no vocational skills or with other employability impairments. If eligible, they could receive UI (or UA if not eligible for UI).

Within the first three weeks of unemployment, the worker's job prospects and vocational improvement needs would be diagnosed and evaluated, and appropriate plans drawn with regard to job search and training or rehabilitation. The job search counselor's views of the job outlook and vocational limitations would be discussed thoroughly and frankly with the unemployed worker. The counselor could encourage the worker to consider seeking jobs quite different from those previously held and to accept lower wages, if necessary, to get started on a new line of work. If a training course is available and appropriate, the worker should be informed of it and encouraged to undertake it. If some other type of rehabilitative measure seems indicated, such as relocation or even some medical therapy to reduce a handicap, that too should be suggested, along with information about the assistance available to enable the worker to take that step. In general, the objective is to give the worker a clear explanation of the probable employment limitations so that a realistic view can develop of what to expect and what course to follow to improve employability.

While on tier 1, the claimant would not have to follow the counselor's suggestions with regard to broadened job search, or to undertake suggested training or other adjustment, since it must be recognized that the counselor's diagnosis is not infallible. This policy would apply especially for a worker affected by a structural dislocation but who feels that there may still be some demand for his or her skills and experience. If, as time goes on, the results of the job search seem indeed to confirm the negative outlook, then the worker should be pressed harder to accept the steps recommended. There should be close monitoring of the worker's job search activity and perhaps several counseling reviews during the first three months of unemployment.

Once beyond tier 1, the unemployed worker who, without good reason, resists consideration of the suggested adjustments should be cautioned that such an attitude may jeopardize eligibility for continued UI protection. If qualified for tier 2, the worker would be paid these benefits with the understanding that payment could be suspended in case of a refusal to accept offers of, or referrals to, different types of jobs or jobs at lower wages than earned previously. If an opportunity for appropriate training or some other rehabilitative measure is refused without good cause after starting to draw tier 2 benefits, the claimant could be disqualified for a period of time. A second disqualification on these grounds would terminate any further UI benefit rights. The same conditions would apply during receipt of tier 3 UI (or of UA).

Job leavers

Workers who voluntarily quit their jobs without good cause and file for UI or UA benefits would be treated in the same manner as those who lose their jobs because of misconduct. A period of benefit suspension would apply, after which they could draw benefits if unemployed and otherwise eligible. They would then be treated about the same as involuntarily separated workers, except that the reason for quitting would be kept in mind for any clues to job search needs or weak labor force attachment.

Pensioners

Under present federal law, workers may not be forced to retire from a job before age 70. Most retire earlier in accordance with collectively bargained agreements or by individual choice. Some workers who go on a pension file for UI benefits. Those who retire voluntarily face the same disqualification as applies for anyone who voluntarily quits the job—retirement is not "good cause." Retirees normally have no difficulty meeting the base-period qualifying requirements for UI, but they must also be able to work, available for work, and actively seeking new employment. Under the JSS, eligible retirees who are unemployed and seek work could qualify for and draw tier 1 benefits provided they meet the current "able and available" conditions.

Federal UI law now requires states to reduce the weekly UI benefit amount by the prorated weekly amount of any retirement pension received by the claimant, including a social security pension, to which a base-period employer has contributed.[2] Most states previously applied a pension reduction, though not for social security. Under the proposed new UI structure, the states would be left free to apply their own rules for tier 1 and tier 2. In tier 3, the federal rule would apply.

Because of their age, pensioners may have above-average difficulty in finding employment, especially employment that is equivalent or similar to their prior jobs. This factor should be taken into account in a diagnosis of the claimant's reemployment prospects and in developing a job search plan, both to be prepared during the first few weeks of filing. Such workers should be urged at this early stage to broaden the range of "suitable" jobs they will seek. Considering the worker's age and receipt of a retirement pension, genuine attachment to the labor force should receive special scrutiny. Inadequate job search and unreasonable restrictions on availability for work, including unjustifiably rigid insistence on defining "suitable work" as only that equivalent to the prior job and wage level, would be grounds for disqualification from UI for a specified period.

Following exhaustion of tier 1 benefits, these workers may qualify for further benefits. The conditions and job services

---

2. The federal pension reduction requirement allows states to take account of the claimant's contributions, if any, to the pension in determining the amount of the reduction.

applicable would be similar to those described for other job losers except that, in general, pensioner claimants must be willing to accept a wider range of jobs, including those paying lower wages, sooner than other job losers. The required reduction of the weekly benefit amount for pensions received, applicable in all states for tier 3, is designed to make lower-paying jobs more attractive when compared to the reduced UI benefit.

Unemployed Persons—Not Previously or Recently Employed

For the most part, this category of the unemployed presents job search problems that differ from those of unemployed workers with recent job experience. New entrants and reentrants to the labor force usually seek work on their own and rely heavily on the suggestions of relatives and friends, and most succeed in finding employment this way. Others make use of specialized services or organizations that have developed to meet their particular needs. These include, for example, school vocational and placement offices for students who have completed their schooling, and agencies that cater to the job search needs of women who have devoted their prior years to homemaking and child rearing and now want paid employment. If low income is a problem, such jobseekers may qualify for employment and training services available through local CETA programs. New entrants and reentrants to the labor force are entitled to register at the Employment Service and the ES can advise them where to obtain specialized assistance beyond what it can offer itself.

Reentrants

Under JSS, some reentrants may meet the minimum qualifying requirements for UI on the basis of employment early in the base period. If so, it would be necessary to learn about the circumstances of the last job separation to determine eligibility for benefits. If the circumstances were disqualifying (a voluntary quit or a misconduct discharge, etc.), a period of benefit suspension would apply. The fact that the worker had dropped out of the labor force for some time would call for careful examination of the reasons for withdrawal and return. If the reentrant is eligible to draw benefits, the benefit reviewer must be alert to any recurrence of similar circumstances that may affect the individual's current availability for work. Apart from these considerations, reentrants who draw UI would be treated the same as other job losers. The treatment would also be the same for reentrants who receive UA instead of UI.

Reentrants who do not qualify for UI or UA may signify their return to the labor force by registering for work at the public employment office. As applicants, they would be entitled to various job services. The type and extent of job search assistance rendered would take account of such considerations as how far back the last employment was; whether it was permanent, temporary, or intermittent employment; whether it was full time or part time; and the type of employment now sought. Apart from need for assistance, the extent of job service provided would depend also on the degree to which current attachment seems permanent and strong.

New entrants

Job applicants with no prior work experience would not be eligible for UI or UA, but they would be entitled to job services. The extent of job services provided would be guided by the new entrant's reasons for entering the labor force, the type of work sought, and the temporary or permanent nature of the individual's current attachment.

Since most new entrants are teenagers, the job search help they need is quite special, particularly for those whose education has been deficient or incomplete, or who suffer from other kinds of deprivation and discrimination. The extremely high rates of minority youth unemployment in our cities is well-known and potentially explosive. In the past, the ES has coped with the job search needs of youth through specialized counseling and other services. In more recent years, youth employment and training programs have proliferated within CETA. Unemployed youths who apply to the JSS for help in seeking their first jobs, or first regular jobs, would be directed to those services, whether within JSS or CETA or elsewhere, that offer the most appropriate course of assistance.

Underemployed Workers

Workers on temporarily reduced work schedules

Workers placed temporarily on a reduced work schedule may be eligible for partial UI for a limited period under the JSS. While drawing partial benefits, they would not be required to register at the employment service or to seek other full-time employment although they would be entitled to do so and to have access to appropriate job services if they wish.

If the reduced work schedule continues beyond the period during which partial benefits are payable, affected workers should be encouraged to register for full-time employment. If they decide voluntarily to leave their jobs at this time to search for full-time work, they would not be disqualified from UI, since the prolonged reduced work schedule can be regarded as good cause for quitting. If they are again offered full-time work by their former employers and they refuse, without good cause, to return to those jobs, they would be disqualified from drawing UI benefits.

Workers seeking other employment

Underemployed full-time workers would not be eligible to receive any UI or UA. They would, however, be entitled to register with the employment service and receive all appropriate assistance in seeking better jobs. The question may arise as to whether they are better off quitting their present jobs so that they can devote more time to seeking new work. In counseling underemployed workers on this question, great care should be taken to avoid recommending that they leave their jobs unless circumstances clearly warrant such action. The pros and cons of doing so should be thoroughly explored along with new job prospects. Underemployed workers should also be informed that quitting because of job dissatisfaction or underemployment could result in a benefit disqualification, although it may not in all cases. For example, if an unemployed worker had taken a job less suitable to his or her skills and experience during a recession while waiting for better job opportunities to open up in the usual field of work, that worker should not be disqualified for quitting to seek such work when prospects improve. Workers who quit because of underemployment would be allowed to take advantage of appropriate training or other vocational adjustment measures that may be available.

IV. EMPLOYMENT SERVICES

How well the JSS responds to the job search needs of its clients depends on the scope of its employment services and the care with which they are applied in individual cases. Not much that is especially new is suggested in the way of particular kinds of services offered. What is new is the greater concentration of effort to bring the available services to bear on the individual jobseeker so as to maximize possibilities for suitable reemployment.

By and large, JSS clients are experienced workers between jobs. Their unemployment is temporary and expected to be limited in duration. Most return to employment without the help of the public employment service, although they generally must register at the ES if they receive income support.

During the last 15 to 20 years, the ES in most places paid less attention than previously to the job search needs of UI claimants, who are experienced workers for the most part. Early in the 1960s, the ES worked to develop a more independent image for itself as a general manpower agency, rather than one that served primarily as an adjunct to UI. Separation of ES from UI took place widely at local levels, both physically and operationally, making the servicing of UI claimant needs more difficult and less likely. The Manpower Development and Training Act of that period expanded the broader manpower responsibilities of the ES, leading it further away from the specific needs of UI claimants. As the 1960s wore on, the consequences of that neglect were not very apparent, since unemployment declined to very low levels. The focus shifted to the treatment and elimination of poverty through training and work experience.

The antipoverty programs of the 1960s created new responsibilities and priorities for the ES, drawing it more heavily into dealing with the employment and training needs of the poor—the "disadvantaged" and the unskilled who had little or unstable work experience, or no work experience at all. In the process, the ES veered from its goal of serving as a general manpower agency. The organization and reorganizations at the federal level of the administration of manpower policies and programs, and associated planning and budgeting functions, did not coincide well with state agency arrangements. Difficulties and confusions resulted at the local levels, along with tensions between the state and federal agencies responsible for the ES. Nor were additional ES responsibilities at the local level matched by sufficient added resources. The ES, consequently, was unable to carry on all of its functions satisfactorily and it drew increasing criticism for its perceived shortcomings.

With the enactment of CETA, the thrust of the 1970s shifted towards local control and organization of employment and training services independent of the state ES agencies. To a great extent, the ES was thereby displaced from the mainstream of this activity. Lack of coordination between the ES and CETA agencies became a major problem. Meanwhile, UI administrators experimented with ways of their own to identify and provide for the needs of claimants for job search assistance in the absence of adequate ES attention in this area.

Serious unemployment reappeared in the 1970s, making more insistent the concerns with UI claimant needs as well as with benefit eligibility issues. The principal response in recent years has been the national effort to implement, within UI operations, the Eligibility Review Program.[1] (This program's title is misleading since it also is intended to cover assistance to claimants in their job search.) The ES has had little or no involvement in this effort.

With regard to the CETA-ES coordination issue, the proposed JSS takes the view that the role of the ES should be more sharply defined as one that deals with the *experienced* unemployed, with workers normally employed on a regular basis but who are temporarily jobless. CETA's concentration is on the inexperienced jobseeker, on the unskilled, on those with the more severe impediments to employability. The rationale for distinguishing between these two sets of clients in this manner is that the type of treatment and services required are generally different. The distinction is not always clear-cut; some overlap is inevitable. For the most part, however, the distinction can be made without much difficulty. Where overlap does occur, coordination between ES and CETA remains necessary. Some JSS clients may benefit by participation in CETA programs and should have access to them. CETA clients, in turn, may in time gain a more established position in the labor force so that subsequent unemployment may bring them under the JSS. Moreover, ES knowledge of the broader labor market could be valuable to CETA clients at some time and should be available to their benefit.

Since experienced unemployed workers are likely to receive UI, the JSS would restore the ES to its earlier, closer association with the UI program. Indeed, the coordination of UI and ES in serving the individual becomes more central than ever. The various kinds of employment services used to help bring about the unemployed worker's reemployment are described separately below. They are, however, to be

---

1. See footnote 1, ch. III.

brought together in an appropriate blend for the individual jobseeker under the direction of the job search counselor.

Placement Services—The Labor Exchange Function

The placement operation of the ES—matching jobseekers and job openings—has been seen right along as its central function and main justification. Each year, ES offices throughout the country place several millions of workers in jobs. The quality and scope of placements vary widely. In some areas, the ES labor exchange function is an important force in the labor market; in others, it is not. Overall, the ES accounts for only a limited fraction of all hirings that occur. That result should not be surprising. Employers are not required to fill their jobs this way, nor are workers compelled to seek jobs through the ES. The prevailing preference is for a free labor market. The ES objective is to help make that market operate more effectively and fairly, not to control it.

A good volume of placement activity is important. The more job orders the ES can fill, the better does it serve the unemployed. If the ES demonstrates to employers that it can supply qualified workers for their labor needs, more employers will turn to it. Workers will also look to the ES for jobs if the openings listed are for desirable jobs. Successful placements can generate increased success on both sides. Too often, however, the ES refers applicants to job openings without adequate preparation to be sure that the match is right and that the job is still open. Employer expectations can be excessive for the existing labor market. It is important that the jobs listed offer realistic wages and working conditions. Job applicants must also be realistic in their expectations. Close counseling of unemployed workers can go far to help assure a reasonable outlook.

Another problem that has emerged over the years that affects ES-employer relations concerns employer apprehensions about the enforcement of public policies to promote equal employment opportunity and affirmative action to achieve it. The ES has certain responsibilities relating to these policies with respect to the job orders it takes and the workers it refers. Application of the rules in a cold, bureaucratic manner can create employer resentment and resistance to using the ES. On the other hand, in a positive and cooperative atmosphere, employers can benefit from working with the ES to ensure that their hiring practices are fair and meet equal employment opportunity objectives. In the final analysis, however, it is the quality of the workers referred to jobs that determines satisfactory service to employers.

Mandatory listing of all job openings has been proposed as a means of strengthening the ES placement function. Employers who supply goods and services under contract to the federal government are now required to list all their job openings with the ES. Little information is available about the use and effectiveness of such listing. Expanded mandatory listing does not seem desirable unless its value can be substantiated. A better course would be to attract more job listings by making more quality placements.

Similarly, not all jobseekers should be required to register with the ES, and no one proposes such a policy. Of course, those who receive UI or other public income support generally must register, although even here there are exceptions. Other jobseekers are less likely to apply to the ES for placement or other services. More of them should be encouraged to do so, including workers currently employed but who believe they are underemployed. Upgrading of the work force is a legitimate goal of the ES, but one that has been neglected. Some employers may not appreciate increased mobility for their workers, and some unions prefer a fairly fixed or limited labor supply in their trades. Employers in general, however, would benefit by having more access to experienced and better skilled workers. Upward movement of such workers also creates more opportunity in vacated jobs for the less experienced and less skilled jobseekers. There is considerable unfilled demand for certain categories of skilled workers.[2] The best supply is presently employed workers who have the desired skills or who can easily develop them. Thus, upgrading could contribute to productivity improvement, a significant current economic goal.

Stress placed on the ES placement function can be overdone. Federal grants to the state agencies to cover their ES administrative costs emphasize placements in the budget allocation formula used. The effect is to encourage quantity rather than quality of placements. Moreover, other important services that do not necessarily lead to ES placements and that may be more difficult to account for adequately for budget purposes may be underfinanced and underemphasized as a result. The budget process should not distort the blend of services needed to promote reemployment, whether achieved directly through the agency's placement function or through some other means. A worker who finds a job on his own as the result of receiving some counseling and job search advice should be regarded as much a success for the agency as is a direct placement. Workers should be encouraged to look for jobs on their own and not to rely entirely on ES job listings. Other services are therefore important to broaden the job search.

Labor Market Information

The ES has the basis for considerable intelligence about the character and dynamics of local labor markets. State employment security agencies have detailed data about

---

2. Even during the 1980 recession, there were serious shortages of skilled workers. See "Who's Minding the Lathe?", an editorial in the *Wall Street Journal,* November 28, 1980 concerning the shortage of machinists.

monthly employment levels by local area, by industry, and even by individual employer, all available from quarterly reports employers submit with their UI tax returns. These reports also indicate the total wages paid out each quarter and, in most states, list all employees and their quarterly earnings. UI operations generate data about the weekly levels of initial claims, indicating new unemployment, and of continued claims filed, the basis of the insured unemployment count. These data are also available by local area. Similarly detailed information derives from ES operations—the number of active job applicants, listed job openings, referrals, placements, etc. Beyond regular operating data, much more information can be drawn from agency records about the characteristics of workers, UI claimants, and job applicants, and their employment and unemployment experience over a period of years. To one degree or another, the state agencies do collect and analyze such information. Local labor market analysts exploit the data for their areas and keep in close touch with events and trends affecting employment and wages on the local scene. While not all the unemployed are reflected in agency records, most of the experienced unemployed are. Nearly all wage and salary employment is reflected, since coverage by UI is almost universal. Local area estimates of total unemployment help account for the probable size of the noninsured segments.

This rich array of data and its analytical potential makes the state agency the obvious source of local labor market information. The degree of exploitation of the data varies considerably by state and by area, depending on the emphasis and resources devoted to this activity and the skills of the analysts. Overall, the data contribute heavily to general economic analysis and policy planning at national and state levels. They are key to state and local planning for CETA programs. Within the context of the primary objectives of the JSS, however, the data's importance lies in how they can help serve the job search needs of individual workers.[3]

Much has been done in organizing the available information in imaginative ways so as to illuminate for jobseekers and job search counselors what is known about jobs and working conditions in the local labor market.[4] Unemployed workers themselves may know a good deal about employment conditions in their particular occupations, especially if they have worked in recent years for different employers in the area. Many, however, are not so knowledgeable. Good labor market information is vital to their job search. It is important that the information be as specific and current as possible. The task of maintaining adequate intelligence centers on the local analyst, but other staff can also contribute to that effort. Local ES office personnel who deal directly with employers and jobseekers pick up bits and pieces of information that can enlarge understanding of current conditions if brought together with other data. Involved staff needs to be highly sensitized to the opportunities their experience affords for improving local labor market information.

The ways in which labor market information can be shaped and applied to be of most use to individual jobseekers have not been adequately explored or developed. Under the JSS, increased counseling to assist individual job search would require more development in this area. An important task of the labor market analyst would be to educate

---

3. For a full description of the data drawn from UI operations and their uses, see "Insured Unemployment Data" by Saul J. Blaustein in "Data Collection, Processing, and Presentation: National and Local," Appendix, Volume II, to *Counting the Labor Force,* a report of the National Commission on Employment and Unemployment Statistics, Washington, DC, September 1979.

4. An excellent example of possibilities along these lines is the *Job Hunter's Guide to Arizona,* Arizona Department of Economic Security, Phoenix, AZ, October 1980. Similar guides are now available for Hawaii and Nevada.

job search counselors about the information available and how it can be used in their work. In time, no doubt, good counselors will themselves determine how best to use the information. While benefit reviewers may be more concerned about the UI claimant's continuing eligibility under the law, they should also have some knowledge of and appreciation for current labor market information. It can help them evaluate more wisely the genuineness of the claimant's job search and attachment, and also whether the claimant needs more or closer job search counseling.

Diagnostic and Counseling Services

While diagnosis of the job search needs and employment prospects of unemployed workers may be more art than science, past experience and various demonstration projects in recent years indicate that reasonable diagnosis is feasible and operationally useful in many, if not most, cases even at the time the individual first registers for work. Moreover, the process stands to gain in effectiveness as improvements accumulate in labor market information, in data about the employability of jobseekers, and in the ability to collate the two through increasingly sophisticated and computerized analysis.[5] Since the diagnostic process is not infallible, periodic reassessment of the jobseeker's situation is necessary when unemployment continues, especially where that reassessment may carry implications for income support eligibility.

5. For evidence and discussion of the application of diagnostic classification to UI claimants, see: David W. Stevens, *Assisted Job Search for the Insured Unemployed* (Kalamazoo, MI: The W.E. Upjohn Institute for Employment Research, January 1974), p. 35 ff; Paul L. Burgess and Jerry L. Kingston, *Unemployment Insurance, the Job Search Process and Reemployment Success* (Washington, DC: U.S. Department of Labor, Employment and Training Administration, Unemployment Insurance Service, June 1974) and David Stevens, *Unemployment Insurance Beneficiary Job Search Behavior: What is Known and What Should Be Known for Administrative Planning Purposes,* UI Occasional Paper Series No. 77-3 (Washington, DC: U.S. Department of Labor, Employment and Training Administration, Unemployment Insurance Service, 1977).

As noted in chapter III, except for those on a temporary layoff, all unemployed workers who file for UI or UA under JSS would receive an initial diagnosis of their reemployment prospects within a few weeks after first filing and registering for work with the ES. The diagnosis would be based primarily on information supplied by each worker on UI and ES forms covering work experience, reasons for job separations, skills, education, training, and other facts relevant to job search, and on current labor market information. As a result of the diagnosis, the worker would be classified as "job ready" or "less readily employable."

The local JSS office would notify workers who are job ready that they should actively seek work in their usual occupations, since employment prospects seem favorable. The notice should invite them to make use of ES facilities and job search aids that are available. It may repeat some information provided when they first filed for benefits or registered at the ES, but a formal communication after a few weeks would serve to emphasize the importance of active job search and to encourage further search. It might also indicate that if no job is found by a specified date, the worker should arrange for a meeting with a job search counselor to discuss methods for seeking work and any problems being encountered. If the worker does not take the initiative to arrange a meeting shortly after the date indicated, the office should do so if the worker is still filing for benefits.

Jobseekers who are diagnosed as less readily employable in their usual jobs, or who have had problems finding or holding jobs before, should be scheduled for a meeting with a job search counselor within two or three weeks of first filing for benefits. The nature of the discussion at this meeting is covered in chapter III (see section on the less employable job seeker). The counselor should summarize the content of the discussion, including any job search plan or other action agreed to, and send a copy to the worker and to the benefit reviewer assigned to the individual. The benefit reviewer would then be responsible for following up with the claimant if the latter is still filing for benefits about a month to six weeks later.

If unemployment continues that long, the benefit reviewer would call in the claimant to go over the results of his or her recent job search activity. The reviewer would determine whether the job search counselor should reassess the worker's prospects and consider other possible steps to take. When unemployment lasts a long time, a periodic review would normally take place about every six to eight weeks and must occur when the claimant files for a new tier of UI benefits or for unemployment assistance. The review process should stress the positive job search objective and not begin primarily as an attempt to determine if the claimant is avoiding employment or is not looking for work with appropriate diligence. The latter information may well emerge from the discussion and lead to a benefit disqualification, but that result is not the initial purpose of the process.

Whether and how often the job search counselor reassesses the worker's situation or classification would depend on the individual's circumstances and labor market conditions. For example, any one or more of the following developments may occasion a reassessment:

a. The job-attached worker may find that the layoff has become permanent or indefinite rather than temporary and short term;

b. The labor market may deteriorate because of a slump in business or some other factor which eliminates favorable job prospects;

c. Labor market information available at the previous assessment may have been inadequate, incorrect, or misinterpreted;

d. The worker's personal circumstances may have changed so as to place obstacles in the path of the job search, or they previously were not accurately reported or were misinterpreted.

A worker classified as job ready may have difficulty finding a job in his or her usual employment. Staff should be alert to possibilities for broadening the worker's range of search by including job possibilities that are not the usual line of work but are close enough to be worth considering. When drawing benefits, the worker can be increasingly encouraged and even subjected to some pressure to broaden the search range, since failure to do so may jeopardize eligibility for benefits. The proposed revised structure for UI is designed to accommodate a reassessment which requires greater flexibility in job search expectations.

With regard to the impact of a general recession on job prospects, it is necessary to recognize that until conditions begin to improve, job-attached or job-ready applicants may continue in these classifications for some time. Periodic reassessments should nevertheless be applied so as not to miss opportunities for broadening the job search when conditions permit. Despite a general recession, favorable job prospects may exist in some areas or in some occupations.

As the process of diagnosis, review, and reassessment is systematically and assiduously applied, it will probably improve and be refined further. Staff should become more skillful as they gain experience in applying the procedures. The labor market information available for the purpose may also improve as needs clarify. To the extent state UI offices are applying the procedures of the current Eligibility Review Program, staff experience will accumulate that can be adapted readily to the JSS procedures. The main difference is the greater intensity and greater emphasis on job search assistance in the JSS approach. The employment service should be more involved in the process. The job search counselor should serve as the link between the ES and the UI or UA programs.

Training and Other Vocational Adjustment Services

Unemployed workers classified as less readily employable reflect a variety of problems, each calling for different treatment. In some cases, the problems and the remedies required are multiple. Despite progress with efforts to establish job readiness, these persons often remain only marginally attractive to employers as workers, especially in loose labor markets. Others may prove to be relatively unyielding to adjustment efforts. Where the obstacles are multiple and deeprooted, the necessary motivation and perseverance may be impossible to sustain. At least at the outset, however, each case should be deemed susceptible of rehabilitation or adjustment. Continued unemployment after some training or other measures may be due as much to inadequate or inappropriate treatment of the individual's problems, or to very limited demand for labor at the time, as it is to his or her own intractability.

It is useful to group the less employable jobseekers into two categories. One includes workers with considerable employment experience, with well-established labor force attachment, but who for one or more reasons have difficulty in finding adequate employment. The other group consists of less experienced workers or workers with unstable employment experience, with inadequate skills, or with physical, emotional, or social handicaps that reduce their employability.

Long-experienced workers

Several types of problems can be identified which cause substantial difficulty and delay in regaining employment for jobseekers with good established work records. One is a deficient understanding of how to look for work. Job search is rarely easy; it may be the hardest task a person faces. Knowing how to look does not come instinctively. Some jobseekers with viable skills and good experience who have not had to seek employment for many years may lack any knowledge about job search techniques. That may be their only obstacle to reemployment, yet it is a serious one. The JSS should be alert to this possibility, especially when reviewing the situations of workers initially classified as job ready but who do not regain employment in a reasonable period of time. Instruction about appropriate job search methods and adequate guidance during the search may be all the remedy needed. Considerable experience has accumulated with regard to job search methodology. Special training or workshops in search techniques and their applications have been shown to be valuable. The JSS should be prepared to supply such service when needed.[6]

Another problem is structural unemployment. Workers who lose their jobs because of a technological change in production techniques which makes their skills obsolete, or who are phased out with the reduction, closure, or relocation of their employers' business activities, are examples of victims of structural unemployment. Unless their skills are transferrable to other fields, they may face long term unemployment. Some are older workers who suffer the additional burden of age discrimination. Retraining is a potential answer. Acquisition of new skills, or the updating or

---

6. For a discussion of developments in counseling and training unemployed workers in job-seeking techniques, see "Job Search Assistance: A Review," by Robert Wegmann in *Journal of Employment Counseling,* December 1979.

upgrading of existing skills, can overcome the problem if there is a demand for those skills in the local labor market. Relocation may be an answer in other cases.

One of the difficulties in prescribing retraining and relocation is that the worker may be unwilling to accept so quickly the need for adjustment, especially if it means the possibility of lower earnings, a long delay in getting back on a regular job, or a disruptive and costly move. Structurally unemployed workers who can benefit from training might be encouraged to move more quickly by offering certain incentives. A supplemental training allowance, on top of the UI benefit, is one possibility; assurance of longer benefit protection to cover the training period and subsequent job search is another.[7] Arrangements might be made with employers for on-the-job training of such workers whereby lower earnings might be supplemented for a time by partial unemployment benefits. Financial assistance may be appropriate to help cover travel and relocation costs and might be supplied to claimants seeking a job in another area or moving to take a job.

Workers laid off because of the adverse effects of foreign competition are also structurally unemployed. Under provisions of the Federal Trade Act of 1974, they may receive Trade Adjustment Allowances which substantially supplement the UI weekly benefit and duration of benefits. They are also eligibile for various adjustment services. Other special programs provide similar benefits for structurally unemployed workers in certain industries.[8] It may be well to generalize on this more generous approach for all workers laid off for structural reasons, particularly if the added

---

7. Michigan provides an extension of UI duration for up to 18 more weeks of benefits to continue the compensation of recipients who are in approved training that lasts beyond the regular UI duration limit.

8. See footnote 5, ch. I.

benefits are made available as inducements to encourage them to undertake adjustments more quickly.

Most training and related remedial measures are currently supplied through CETA-sponsored programs. Income and other requirements may bar entry for structurally unemployed workers. Moreover, their training needs may be quite different from those of the usual CETA program enrollees. JSS should arrange for training and other adjustment services designed for the experienced unemployed who need assistance to maintain their viability in a changing labor market.

Some workers, after years of steady and satisfactory employment, run into difficulties because of emerging personal problems that may be unrelated to their vocational abilities but which interfere with their ability to perform on the job. They may lose their jobs as a result. Without some outside help, they may be unable to resolve their problems, which can include the onset of bad health, family instability, and emotional breakdown. Alcoholism and drug abuse are other examples which loom large. The JSS should work with employers to arrange referrals of such workers to community agencies that can help in an effort to prevent the problem from getting out of hand and to forestall layoffs. If the worker does lose the job, the JSS should try to identify the problem and support efforts to resolve it. Where needed, some financial assistance should be available to help pay the costs of medical or counseling services obtained to deal with these problems.

Other less readily employable jobseekers

An important part of this category consists of unemployed youths, particularly those who recently graduated from school or left school before completion. Many eventually work their way into regular employment after some trial and error experience, and that is not necessarily an objectionable process. The process, however, is often disorganized, inefficient, and more prolonged than necessary. The problem is not so much a matter of finding jobs, but rather one of obtaining appropriate regular or stable employment which enables young workers to develop good experience and skills. They can usually work enough to meet the work or earnings qualifying requirements for UI and therefore enter the JSS in this way. In many instances, however, they are disqualified for UI because they quit jobs.

In the past, the public employment services have attempted to supply guidance in one way or another to ease the transition from school to work. The means employed include special counseling and placement services for youths, and the promotion of vocational guidance in the schools. These efforts have been neither universal nor continuous. It is important to build a strong, steady program of vocational guidance covering all senior and junior high schools and involving a close active working relationship between JSS and school staff. Students should be exposed early and often to instruction about the realities of work, occupations, careers, and job search techniques. When youngsters do apply for help at a JSS office, the system should be prepared to work closely with them, on a long-range basis if necessary, until a pattern of regular, stable employment is established.

CETA training and work experience programs focus heavily on young people with the more difficult problems that are frequently associated with poverty and discrimination. Disadvantaged, ill-educated youths from poor households are especially in need of vocational preparation, and many CETA programs are designed for them. These include the Job Corps and newer programs authorized by the Youth Employment and Demonstration Projects Act of 1977. Low family income is usually a prerequisite, and a training allowance may be provided in some cases. Most young people who enroll in a CETA program do so directly, without first applying at the public employment office. Those who do apply at the ES and who may qualify for CETA should be referred to the CETA agency.

A somewhat similar set of employment problems exists for women who reenter the labor force after lengthy absence. Most find jobs on their own. Others may need some guidance or assistance in establishing a regular employment pattern. If they apply for benefits or services under the JSS, they should receive appropriate treatment. Special training or work-preparation programs are emerging more widely for homemakers planning to seek employment or who have worked part-time or sporadically and now want regular work. The JSS should refer them to such programs where they are available, or help to form one as needed. CETA may also be dealing with these needs, and the JSS should cooperate and participate in developing the appropriate services, since not all the women who can benefit are eligible for CETA assistance.

Coordination with CETA would be especially important for JSS if the proposed unemployment assistance program is established. Women now on AFDC who are expected to be available for work would, in many cases, qualify for UA; some might qualify for UI after some work experience. As is now the case with WIN, the state agency would be responsible under JSS to supply or arrange for vocational adjustment assistance for these women to enhance their employability. Some training and other work experience programs provided through CETA could be used or adapted for the purpose. In addition to the lack of job skills and experience, non-vocationally-related personal problems are also likely to be present among this group. Poor health, emotional instability, family disruption, alcoholism, unreliable child care arrangements, and other difficulties may have to be treated before, or along with, vocational preparation. Some community resources may be available to such individuals, and they should be encouraged to turn to them for help. Often those resources are limited or not accessible for the unemployed. JSS and CETA should seek expansion of and greater accessibility to such assistance.

The objective of WIN and related efforts is to bring such people into increasing self-support, weaning them away from welfare. "Graduation" to unemployment assistance or UI, after some job experience, may signify an important forward step in the process. The JSS should be prepared to supply continuing guidance and remedial services in these cases until the worker becomes well-established and self-sustaining.

Another group of less readily employable jobseekers consists of underemployed workers, particularly those who work part-year in seasonal jobs and who want year-round employment. Many draw unemployment benefits in the off season. The JSS would diagnose such benefit recipients for possible preparation for year-round jobs and encourage or even require them to undertake appropriate training or work experience as a condition for continued benefits.

Job Creation and Subsidized Employment

Although not assumed as a function of the JSS, the creation and funding of a large number of temporary public service jobs has become, under CETA, a major strategy for alleviating long term structural and cyclical unemployment. CETA specifies essentially two types of public service employment. One (under Title II of the Act) emphasizes the work experience or training aspect of the job for structurally unemployed and other less readily employable jobseekers. The intent is to enable the individual placed in the job to move into regular employment as the result of the experience. The other type of public service employment (Title

VI) supplies work opportunities during recession periods when normal jobs are temporarily curtailed. Instead of drawing income support for prolonged periods, the unemployed worker can use the time to render a productive public service that might not otherwise be performed. The scope and volume of public service employment may face restriction in coming years.[9]

New jobs are also created for the unemployed in the private sector through federally funded expansion of public works concentrated in high-unemployment areas and during periods of heavy unemployment. Moreover, there are now special federal tax credits available under certain conditions to employers who hire persons from particularly disadvantaged groups, such as low-income youth, Vietnam veterans, and handicapped individuals.[10] These credits represent a portion of the wages paid to such workers. In addition, stronger efforts are being made in other ways to engage private industry more in dealing with long term and hard-core unemployment by developing more training and work experience opportunities in private sector jobs.[11]

The major expansion in jobs for the unemployed during recent years of high unemployment has come in CETA-funded public service employment. By and large, JSS clients would not be likely to qualify for such jobs unless they have remained unemployed for a long period of time (for at least

9. Public service employment has become increasingly criticized as a countercyclical measure for coming on too late, for staying on too long, for substituting for state and local funding of regular government jobs instead of financing new jobs, for supporting unproductive work, and for poor management. It is also criticized for being inadequate considering the large numbers of unemployed who are unable to find regular jobs in relatively good times as well as bad, and for an inadequate variety of types of work experience in jobs provided under Title II.

10. The Targeted Jobs Tax Credit program was established under the Revenue Act of 1978.

11. The efforts include support under Title VII of CETA for a Private Sector Initiatives Program (PSIP) and local Private Industry Councils to help plan and promote PSIP, and the increasing involvement of private sector employers in local employment service advisory committees under the Job Service Improvement Program.

15 weeks) and are from low-income households. When clients are eligible, the JSS should consider referrals to those jobs, as appropriate.

Working temporarily, even at something less rewarding or desirable than what the worker wanted or usually did, should be considered preferable to long term income support, provided it is useful work. Prolonged idleness may undermine the unemployed worker's self-respect and basic attachment to the labor force, as well as normal work habits and discipline. Created temporary employment of this nature provides the JSS with another means for protecting the security of workers as workers. With adequate advance planning, there is probably much in the way of worthwhile work that could be accomplished through this means that would not otherwise be done.

Recent welfare reform proposals also emphasize the creation of more public service jobs to assure the substitution of work for welfare for those able to work. This policy would operate to shift employable AFDC recipients into an increasingly solid attachment to the labor force. Job security, rather than income security, would become the primary means for assuring their welfare. The establishment of an unemployment assistance program, as proposed under JSS, would carry this concept even further. Temporary public service and private sector jobs would serve as an important means for guiding UA recipients toward self-supporting regular employment.

Because of the widespread criticism of public service employment in recent years and the way the political climate has shifted toward less enthusiasm for that approach, more emphasis is likely to be given in the future to private sector initiatives. Broadening the present limited job tax credit program or developing other types of public wage subsidies could aim at expanding on-the-job training or work experience opportunities in private industry. That approach can enlarge the variety of training and experience beyond what is possible in public service jobs and enhance prospects for regular permanent employment in the private sector. Care must be taken to be sure that employers do not use the subsidies to replace regular workers by subsidized workers, comparable to the substitution effect encountered with public service employment.

V. THE THREE-TIER
UNEMPLOYMENT INSURANCE PROGRAM

The elements of the Job Security System which would modify present arrangements most significantly are the income support programs. Unemployment insurance would be substantially restructured and a new unemployment assistance program would be established. This chapter discusses the proposed reform of UI; chapter VI discusses UA.

The Present UI Structure

The existing federal-state UI system, now over 45 years old, has much the same basic framework with which it began. Each state has its own program defined by its own statutory provisions. The state is responsible for raising its own funds to finance the benefits it pays. State UI provisions specify the qualifying requirements, eligibility conditions, and the weekly amount and duration of benefits payable. Except for a few federal requirements applicable largely to eligibility rules, each state determines its own benefit provisions. These vary considerably among states as a result. Federal UI law has more influence over state UI benefit financing, but even here each state has wide latitude in setting UI tax rates and the level of reserves it maintains. In effect, federal law prohibits a state from setting its employer tax rates below 2.7 percent of taxable payrolls except on the basis of experience rating.[1] All states, therefore, provide experience-rated taxes,[2] but taxes on employers with similar experience can and do vary greatly among the states. The federal government has even more impact on the administration of the program, mainly because it finances administrative costs through annual grants to the states out of revenues from the Federal Unemployment Tax (FUT) on employer payrolls. There are also a number of statutory federal requirements with which the states must comply in the administration of their laws.

Two important features have been added to the program's basic structure since it began. One is a provision for federal loans to states with exhausted benefit reserves to enable them to continue paying benefits. Repayable, interest-free advances may be obtained by such states from a federal loan fund accumulated out of FUT revenues. The borrowing state must repay after about two to three years, or have its debt reduced in annual installments through reductions in the tax credit its employers can take each year against the federal unemployment tax.[3] If the federal loan fund is insufficient to meet all needs, it may draw repayable advances from the U.S. Treasury.[4]

The other added feature is the provision of extended benefits (EB) during periods of high unemployment. Enacted in 1970, the EB program provides for a 50 percent

---

1. A Federal Unemployment Tax (currently 3.4 percent), which applies to each covered employer's taxable payroll, may be offset by the amount of state UI tax the employer pays, up to 2.7 percent of payroll; if the employer pays less than 2.7 percent to the state, an additional tax credit is allowed against the federal tax to cover the difference (i.e., the full 2.7 percent credit may be taken) if the state tax was reduced on the basis of the unemployment experience of the employer's work force.

2. Except for Puerto Rico, considered a "state" in the UI system.

3. See footnote 1 explaining the tax credit.

4. The federal loan fund accumulates up to a limit of $550 million, which was well short of needs in the mid-1970s.

extension of the regular benefit duration payable to claimants under the state law, up to a 39-week maximum for regular benefits and EB combined. Extensions trigger on automatically when state or national insured unemployment rates exceed specified levels, and trigger off when they fall below those levels. Each state is responsible for financing half the costs of the EB it pays; the other half is financed by the federal government out of an account accumulated for the purpose from FUT revenues. If this account is depleted, as was the case in the mid-1970s, it is replenished by repayable U.S. Treasury advances. In effect, then, the existing federal-state UI system is a two-tiered program—a basic tier of regular state benefits generally compensating up to the first 26 weeks of unemployment and, for those exhausting regular benefits when unemployment is high, a second tier of federal-state shared EB covering up to 13 additional weeks of unemployment to an overall maximum of 39 weeks.[5]

In 1971 and in 1974, Congress provided for temporary supplemental benefit programs for the recessions then in progress. While they lasted, these programs provided additional weeks of benefits for claimants who exhausted EB—up to another 13 weeks under each program, and up to 26 more weeks for a while during the later program, with overall potential maximums of 52 and 65 weeks of benefits. All the costs of these supplemental benefits—in effect, a third tier—were wholly federally financed, at first out of FUT revenues, but later from general revenues. These benefits were payable only in states where the insured unemployment trigger rate reached specified levels. During 1980, Congress again considered but did not adopt a tem-

5. In most states, many claimants who exhaust regular benefits draw less than the 26 weeks maximum and therefore are entitled to fewer than 13 weeks of EB, i.e., less than 39 weeks in all, when EB is payable. Some states pay regular benefits for more than 26 weeks. During EB periods, the federal government pays half the cost of regular benefits paid after the 26th week—the overall 39-week limit still applies in these states.

porary third tier of federal supplemental benefits (FSB) for the current recession.

On the whole, the existing federal-state UI system has functioned well, at least until recent years when it ran into serious financial difficulties. The program has had and continues to have its weaknesses and inadequacies, but it has never failed to pay the benefits provided under the laws. Each year, UI helps to sustain the incomes of millions of jobless workers during periods of temporary unemployment. In many communities hit hard by unemployment, benefit outlays uphold the purchasing power needed to keep local business going and to help prevent further deterioration. After 45 years, UI has become generally well accepted as an important and necessary institution in our society.

Duration and Financing Problems and the National Commission

UI, however, does have its problems. The program has always been issue-prone, and controversy has swirled almost continuously about many of its features. Moreover, the economic setting in which it operates changes constantly. Without adequate evolution over a long period of time in response to such change, the program can grow less responsive to current needs. Many observers feel that UI has not evolved enough over the years to avoid that result.

The severe recession of the mid-1970s jolted the UI system and left it in a good deal of financial disarray. Almost half the states exhausted their reserves and had to borrow from the federal loan fund. Total state borrowing reached to over $5.5 billion by the end of 1978, most of which had to be advanced to the system from general revenues. In addition, general revenue advances were needed to support federal EB and FSB costs. The system's outstanding obligations to the

U.S. Treasury for all advances totaled about $12.5 billion in late 1980. About half the borrowing states repaid all of their loans by 1980 and others have repaid part. With another recession in progress, more financial difficulties threaten to compound the problem. Further borrowing by states has occurred in 1980 and early in 1981. Outstanding state indebtedness totaled about $5 billion at the close of 1980.[6]

The FSB extensions, which carried benefit duration beyond 39 weeks, and even beyond 52 weeks for a time, have raised serious questions in some quarters about the UI program's integrity as a form of insurance against temporary unemployment. Use of general revenues to finance FSB breaks out of the traditional pattern of self-contained financing for UI which has been widely regarded as an important feature of the program's insurance character. These benefits were perceived by many observers more as welfare payments than as insurance benefits based on earned rights.

The program's problems, along with its financial crisis in the mid-1970s, combined to induce Congress to authorize, for the first time, a national commission devoted entirely to a study of the UI system and its problems. The National Commission on Unemployment Compensation (NCUC) carried out its comprehensive review of the program from early 1978 through the summer of 1980. Its *Final Report,* of July 1980, contains its findings, conclusions, and recommendations. The NCUC's recommendations are wide-ranging, covering all aspects of UI as well as some features of other programs bearing on UI, such as the public employment service and special federal unemployment benefit programs for particular groups of workers, e.g., Trade Readjustment Assistance. The recommendations vary in the degree of

---

6. Information about state UI loans and general U.S. Treasury advances based on data supplied to the author by the Unemployment Insurance Service of the U.S. Department of Labor's Employment and Training Administration.

agreement they commanded among Commission members, ranging from unanimous to very narrow support.

Some observations are appropriate here about two areas of the Commission's work and recommendations—those relating to benefit duration and to financing—since these are two of the UI problem areas to which the proposed new three-tier program is addressed.

The Commission chose not to recommend alteration of the program's basic structure. It suggested that the states continue to be fully responsible for regular benefits up to at least 26 weeks maximum duration. A NCUC majority did support federal minimum benefit standards, however, including one affecting the amount of base-period employment states may require to qualify for 26 weeks of regular benefits. This standard specifies that a state may not require a claimant to have more than 39 weeks of base-period employment (or an equivalent amount and spread of base-period earnings) to be eligible for 26 weeks of benefits. The Commission also urged a gradual reduction of the 39 weeks employment limit but did not specify how much lower it should be eventually. The initial level of the standard would eliminate the most extreme duration restrictions currently applicable in several states but would leave many states with large proportions of claimants qualifying for less than 26 weeks of protection. In 1979, there were 27 states where 40 percent or more of all eligible claimants could not qualify for 26 weeks of benefits and 34 states where over half the claimants who exhausted regular benefits drew for less than 26 weeks.[7] Adoption of the proposed standard would probably not alter these patterns much until the qualifying requirement limit is reduced substantially.

The Commission also recommended retention of the triggered EB program for high unemployment periods, carrying

---

7. *Unemployment Insurance Statistics,* October-December 1979, pp. 54 and 56.

benefit duration to an overall maximum of 39 weeks. No change was suggested in the 50 percent extension of the individual claimant's regular benefit entitlement or in the federal-state sharing of EB costs. A few improvements were recommended in the EB trigger mechanism. The discussion of several other issues relating to EB did not lead to recommendations for change.

The basic approach of using a statistical indicator to trigger EB sometimes produces odd and arbitrary borderline results that may not be intended. Statistics on insured unemployment are not so precise or accurate as to assure that EB will always trigger on and off at the right time and in the right place.[8] Wide variation among and within states in the severity of unemployment has led to some questioning of the policy of EB payments triggering on nationwide, and even statewide, and to proposals to eliminate the national trigger and to trigger EB on a local basis. The NCUC was evenly divided on the former proposal and rejected the latter. Locally triggered EB seems not at all feasible because it poses extremely difficult technical problems of statistical measurement and administration. Another EB concern has been with the combined long duration of benefits that claimants with very limited base-period employment can receive in some states, e.g., qualifying for 39 weeks of benefits with 20 or fewer weeks of employment. The Commission discussed but did not recommend a higher minimum qualifying requirement for EB.

A majority favored a permanent standby program of FSB, triggered on a national and state basis. The program would provide up to two additional segments, each equal to 50 percent of the claimant's regular benefit entitlement and subject to a 13-week limit. Successively higher trigger thresholds

---

8. Seasonal adjustment of the state trigger rates, as recommended by the NCUC, would be an important improvement in this regard.

would apply for each FSB segment, as compared with EB trigger thresholds, and the overall duration ceilings would be 52 and 65 weeks, respectively. The FSB benefits would be wholly federally financed out of general revenues. There was less support for the second FSB segment and for paying FSB on a national triggered basis.

Commission majorities supported more change when it came to UI financing. Recommendations included increasing the federal taxable wage base, charging interest on loans made to the states from the federal loan fund, and advice to the states regarding the maintenance of solvent reserve funds. Another significant recommendation was to establish a reinsurance plan that would make grants to states from a nationally pooled fund to ease part of the very heavy cost burdens some states experience during recession periods. The Commission did not endorse any of the specific reinsurance plans that have been advanced, but it did indicate a few parameters which a majority favored. The plan was to be modest, financed by a fund accumulated out of FUT revenue allocations equal at first to no more than 0.1 percent of taxable payrolls each year. Reinsurance grants to eligible states would cover no more than 30 percent of defined excess costs, and less if accumulated reinsurance funds available for a given year were insufficient to meet the 30 percent level. To be eligible for a grant, a state's benefit costs for a given period must equal or exceed 2.7 percent of taxable payrolls.

The way a reinsurance plan defines excess cost or eligibility conditions for a grant tends to pit one group of states against another. Alternative definitions or conditions can have very different effects on which states qualify and for how much. The Commission's recommended minimum requirement of a 2.7 percent cost rate would probably preclude a number of states from receiving grants because they always have had relatively low rates of insured unemployment and benefit costs. Those states object to having their employers contribute to a fund from which they are very unlikely to benefit. Under another approach, a minimum percentage increase in benefit cost or insured unemloyment levels between one period and another would qualify a state for a grant regardless of the absolute level of these measures. High-cost states object to this idea because they may not be able to qualify on that basis. One proposed plan would combine both the absolute level of the insured unemployment rate and the percentage increase in order to broaden support among the states. Designing an adequate reinsurance plan that would command a broad political base among the states remains problematical.

Features of the Proposed Three-Tier Program

The proposed new UI structure would attack, directly, the duration and financing problems of the present UI program. First, the new program would not go beyond the 39th week of unemployment. Second, all UI benefits would be financed by state and federal employer payroll taxes with no resort to general revenues. The proposed financing arrangements would reduce the likelihood of state fund insolvency.

The proposed program is divided into three segments or tiers, each providing uniform potential duration of 13 weeks of benefits. Each tier is governed by different eligibility conditions and financed by a different mix of state and federal taxes. The third tier, which carries benefit protection up to 39 weeks, would be available at all times and would not be dependent on a triggering mechanism tied to the unemployment level.

The 39-week limit

The justification for the 39-week limit derives from the basic financing concept underlying UI in this country, the empirical experience regarding the adequacy of UI duration provisions, and the availability of other forms of assistance for those beyond the protection of UI.

A fundamental principle applying to UI in the United States is that its costs should be absorbed by business. By this approach, the costs are allocated to production and in turn subject to the discipline of the market-price system. Charging UI costs to employers also motivates them to minimize or avoid laying off their workers. The application of this principle explains the virtually exclusive reliance on employer payroll taxes to support the program and the experience rating of those taxes.[9] With such financing, some limit on the maximum potential liability of individual employers is appropriate, and limiting benefit duration seems a reasonable means for accomplishing it. Also, a duration limit appears appropriate within this context in that, as unemployment continues for a very long time, the link between UI benefits paid as a matter of earned rights and the prior employment on which they are based becomes increasingly tenuous, and the benefits paid become less justifiable as the financial responsibility of employers.

The present UI program began modestly with respect to benefit duration out of fear of excessive costs. As it became clear that the program's financial base could support longer duration, states gradually raised their duration limits to 26 weeks, some even beyond that level. The objective for the duration provision was that UI benefits should be payable long enough to carry the great majority of recipients through their unemployment. This view focuses attention on exhaustees—claimants whose unemployment lasts beyond the UI duration limit.

Historically, the tendency for claimants to exhaust benefits at given levels of unemployment has related closely to the statutory limits placed on benefit duration. As states

---

9. Only 3 states derive some revenues from employee taxes to help finance UI.

improved their benefit duration provisions, the rate of exhaustion declined. Since 1960, when the national average potential duration of regular state benefits reached 24 weeks, about where it has remained, the national exhaustion rate has ranged between 18 and 38 percent, varying primarily by the rate of unemployment (table 2). Among the states, exhaustion rates vary over a wider range, reflecting variations in both the duration allowed and the rate of unemployment. Generally, the more restricted the duration allowed, the higher the exhaustion rate.

The regular state duration provisions, as a whole, carry a large proportion of claimants (about 75 to 80 percent) through their unemployment only when the insured unemployment rate has been about 3 percent or less. During the 1970s, unemployment was higher, and so was the number of exhaustions of regular benefits. During recession periods, EB comes into play, extending potential duration by half. During the 1970s, about 65 percent of claimants who drew EB exhausted those benefits.[10] At that rate, regular and EB duration combined appeared adequate to carry about 75 to 80 percent of all UI recipients through their unemployment, even during periods of high unemployment. The combined limit of 39 weeks of benefits comes close to achieving the objective of carrying the great majority through their unemployment.

Even so, the numbers exhausting EB during the recession years of the mid-1970s were large—2.5 million in 1975, 2.4 million in 1976, and 1.8 million in 1977—large enough to explain the FSB extensions during this period. The only alternative for EB exhaustees is welfare—AFDC or state or local general assistance. These programs, however, are quite restrictive, so that many EB exhaustees who are in need of

---

10. Based on total final EB payments from 1970 to 1978 as a percent of first EB payments, 1970 to mid-1978.

Table 2
Potential Duration of Benefits, Exhaustion Rate, and Insured
Unemployment Rate under Regular State UI Programs
U.S. Averages, 1960-1978

Year	Average potential duration of regular benefits (weeks)	Exhaustion rate[1] (percent)	Insured unemployment rate[2] (percent)
1960	24.0	26.1	4.7
1961	23.9	30.4	5.7
1962	23.9	27.4	4.3
1963	24.1	25.3	4.2
1964	24.2	23.8	3.7
1965	24.1	21.5	2.9
1966	24.2	18.0	2.2
1967	24.5	19.3	2.4
1968	24.3	19.6	2.2
1969	24.4	19.8	2.1
1970	24.6	24.4	3.4
1971	24.5	30.5	4.1
1972	23.8	28.9	3.0
1973	24.3	27.6	2.5
1974	24.4	31.2	3.4
1975	24.3	37.8	6.1
1976	24.0	37.8	4.4
1977	24.1	33.4	3.7
1978	24.5	26.8	2.8

SOURCE: *Handbook of Unemployment Insurance Financial Data,* 1938-1976, and Annual Supplements, U.S. Department of Labor, Employment and Training Administration.

1. Claimants receiving final payments in calendar year as a percent of claimants receiving first payments in a 12-month period ending 6 months earlier.

2. Insured unemployed workers as a percent of covered employment.

further income support cannot qualify for welfare. AFDC is not available for families without dependent children and, in about half the states, for families in which both parents are present. Without an adequate back-up program for workers who need further support for a time, the pressures to extend UI beyond 39 weeks are almost irresistable during recession years. The UA program of the proposed JSS would relieve those pressures. The National Commission on Unemployment Compensation recommended the establishment of a UA program, although it also recommended FSB extensions beyond 39 weeks for recession periods.

Financing

Under the proposed UI program, the financing arrangement for each tier would vary by the mix of state and federal responsibility, although all financing would rely on employer payroll taxes levied for the purpose. Presently, each state finances its regular UI benefits from its own UI reserve fund accumulated from experience-rated employer payroll taxes.[11] EB costs are shared equally by state UI reserves and the federal UI trust fund account reserved for extended benefits. In about half the states, the state pools its share of EB costs among all its employers; the rest experience rate those costs. The federal share of EB costs is pooled nationally among all covered employers.

Under the proposed three-tier program, the states would be totally responsible for tier 1 costs and probably would continue to experience rate these costs. In the sense that experience rating reflects the notion that an individual firm bears the responsbility for the unemployment of its employees, the full experience rating of short term benefits is logical. Much unemployment is short term and more likely

---

11. Some added revenues are raised from employee taxes in three states; Puerto Rico does not experience rate.

than longer term unemployment to be controllable, to some extent, by the employer. One objective of experience rating is to encourage employers to minimize unemployment; tier 1 is the most appropriate segment in which to concentrate that effect.

Tier 2 costs would be shared equally between state and federal UI reserve funds, as is now the case with EB costs. As unemployment moves beyond the short term range of tier 1, the responsbility of the individual firm for the unemployment of its employees grows more and more remote. National pooling of half the costs of tier 2 benefits acknowledges that the continued unemployment is less subject to employer control and more likely to be the result of broader forces that are multi-state or national in scope. The states would be able to choose between pooling or experience rating the state share of tier 2 costs, as is now the arrangement for state EB costs.

An extension of the argument for increased pooling of tier 2 costs leads to support for total national pooling of the UI costs for the much longer unemployment involved in tier 3. Federal UI funds would finance all tier 3 benefits.

The three-tier financing arrangement would have two important effects. One would be to reduce the scope of experience rating. While limited to short term tier 1 benefits and, if the state chooses, half the costs of tier 2, experience rating would still apply for most of the UI benefit costs of the first 26 weeks of unemployment. Three-tier cost estimates, to be discussed below, indicate that tier 1 benefit costs plus half the costs of tier 2 would account for about 70 to 75 percent of all UI costs under the proposed program. Tier 1 alone would account for about 60 percent of all costs. Thus, experience rating would still play a substantial role.

Depending on how a state redesigns its UI tax structure, confining experience rating to tier 1 costs might provide a better opportunity to effectively charge all, or nearly all, such costs to individual employers. At present, a portion of benefit costs charged to some high-cost employers is not covered by their taxes because of maximum tax rates. The range of existing tax schedules is likely to make experience rating more completely effective for short term benefit costs. Employers with seasonal operations that generate a great deal of short term but little longer term insured unemployment often are at the maximum rate, but some are ineffectively charged for all costs. To the extent these employers have tier 2 and 3 costs which are pooled through a uniform tax, the experience-rated taxes they now pay at maximum tax rates would cover more, if not all, of their short term UI costs.

One other advantage claimed for experience rating, that of involving employers in verifying the legitimacy of claims for UI entitlement, would be maintained adequately by the charging of tier 1 benefits to the separating employer. Since the cooperation of employers in checking the legitimacy of claims concerns mainly job separation issues, the employers' stake in tier 1 benefits would still motivate them to identify claims that should be disqualified.

The second effect of the three-tier financing arrangement derives from the expanded national pooling of UI costs—half the benefits of tier 2 and all of tier 3. To a considerable extent, the broader pooling would accomplish the objective of reinsurance without having to establish a special scheme for the purpose. All the reinsurance or cost equalization plans advanced so far face a dilemma. Either they discriminate against low-cost states by concentrating the reinsurance or cost equalization grants among the high-cost states, or they allow all states a chance to qualify for grants without regard to the levels of costs or to unemployment levels, thereby reducing the grants to high-cost states needed to offset their "excess costs." Schemes that attempt to strike a balance between these two positions often involve complex mechanisms to determine state eligibility for grants and the amounts of the grants payable. National pooling of half of tier 2 and all of tier 3 costs would relieve all states of some cost burden, and would relieve the high-unemployment, high-cost states of a larger proportion of their total burden. High unemployment levels usually mean longer duration of unemployment and, therefore, proportionately more tier 2 and tier 3 benefits. National pooling of costs in these tiers would ease the strains on state UI financing and offer better assurance of fund solvency.

Qualifying requirements and potential duration

Under their present UI laws, all states require a minimum amount of employment and/or earnings in a base period to qualify for any benefits.[12] These minimum requirements vary a good deal among the states, both in form and level. As of January 1981, 13 states rquired from 14 to 20 weeks of employment to qualify. Except for Washington, which specified a minimum number of hours of work (680) in the base period, all other states stated their requirements in terms of earnings. For 16 states, total base-period earnings had to equal at least a specified multiple of earnings in the highest quarter, ranging from 1.25 to 1.6. If the claimant had 13 weeks of work in the high quarter, this range of multiples was equivalent to a little more than 16 to nearly 21 weeks of work in the base period, provided the weekly amount earned was constant. Another 16 states required total earnings equal to at least a specified multiple of the weekly benefit amount for which the claimant qualified,

---

12. State UI provisions as of January 1981 are from *Comparison of State Unemployment Insurance Laws* and *Significant Provisions of State Unemployment Insurance Laws,* January 4, 1981, both issued by the U.S. Department of Labor's Employment and Training Administration.

which in turn depended on the level and fraction of high-quarter earnings used to calculate the weekly benefit amount and on the benefit ceiling. The equivalence of this type of requirement to weeks of employment is less consistent than that of the high-quarter multiple. To the extent the claimant's employment pattern is that needed to make them equivalent, the weekly benefit multiples, ranging generally from 30 to 40, would be equivalent to about 15 to 20 weeks of work. The remaining states required a minimum flat amount of base-period earnings, from $600 to $1,400, usually with earnings required in at least two quarters. Work time equivalents are indeterminate for these requirements, but flat-earnings tests make it possible to qualify with considerably less than 14 weeks of work.

These minimum requirements qualify a claimant for a given level of potential duration, usually the minimum in the states which vary the weeks allowed by the base-period experience. As of January 1981, 43 states varied the duration allowed; in the other states, all eligible claimants qualified for a uniform potential duration. Minimum potential duration in the variable duration states ranged from 4 to 20 weeks. Because of the variation in the duration formulas used by these states, the number of weeks of employment (or the equivalent in earnings) needed by claimants to qualify for 26 weeks of benefits ranged widely. In several states, only claimants who worked all 52 weeks in their base periods could qualify for 26 weeks; in a few others, only 26 weeks of employment were needed.[13] Among the uniform duration states, claimants qualified for 26 or 28 weeks of benefits with as few as 14 to 20 weeks of work (or the equivalent) in most, and with the flat minimum amount of base-period earnings

---

13. In 1980, Pennsylvania replaced its 30-week uniform duration provision by one providing up to 26 weeks of benefits to claimants with at least 18 weeks of base-period employment and up to 30 weeks for those who worked at least 24 weeks.

required to qualify in a few others.[14] Eight states provided more than 26 weeks of regular benefits with duration maximums ranging from 28 to 36 weeks among them; they required more base-period employment to qualify for the longer duration (except for one uniform duration state). During EB periods, the potential duration that claimants can draw is 50 percent more (up to a 39-week overall maximum) without any additional base-period employment required. Among the uniform duration states, this means that claimants with as little as 14 to 20 weeks of employment could qualify for 39 weeks of benefits during EB periods.

The three-tier program would alter this pattern. The qualifying requirements (except for tier 1) and the potential duration allowed in each tier would be the same in all states. Each tier would provide a uniform potential duration of 13 weeks, but the total number of weeks allowed claimants by the program would vary with their past employment. The three levels of total potential duration—13, 26, and 39 weeks—are associated with three levels of qualifying requiremets, which may be more or less than present state requirements for these levels of potential duration. All three tiers would be available at all times, without regard to the level of unemployment.

Since tier 1 would be financed entirely by the states, they would set the qualifying requirements for these benefits. The requirements for tiers 2 and 3 would be set by federal law; these may induce the states to adopt tier 1 requirements that would be consistent with them.It may be desirable, however, to set a federal standard limiting the *range* of tier 1 requirements. No state now requires more than about 20 weeks of base-period employment (or the equivalent) to qualify for minimum benefits.The preferred requirement for tier 1 would fall between 14 and 20 weeks of base-period employment, measured directly in weeks. A high-quarter multiple

---

14. Puerto Rico provides only 20 weeks of uniform duration.

requirement would be acceptable as an equivalent if it fell in the range of 1.1 and 1.5. The weekly benefit amount multiple and, especially, the flat earnings requirements would not be acceptable as equivalents.

For tier 2, the qualifying requirement would be 26 weeks of base-period employment, or annual earnings equal to twice high-quarter earnings. Because of federal financial participation in tier 2 benefits with funds raised by a uniform tax nationwide, it is appropriate to set a uniform require-ment. The same reasoning applies for tier 3. Most states now require more than 26 weeks of work (or the equivalent) for potential duration of 26 weeks; the majority require about 39 or more weeks.

The tier 3 qualifying requirement would be 39 weeks of base-period employment (or an acceptable high-quarter-multiple earnings equivalent), but with an alternative of 52 weeks of work in the past 104 weeks (base period and the preceding year combined). In a period of recession, a 39-week requirement may be difficult to meet. A claimant who normally works most of the time but who had substan-tial unemployment during the previous year or lost time due to illness should be able to qualify for the third tier if his prior work record indicates good regular attachment. The alternative allows that opportunity.

One other problem with present qualifying requirements concerns the minimum amount of earnings specified per week, or per quarter, or per year. For states using a weeks-of-work test, a minimum amount of earnings per week is re-quired (in a few states, a minimum average per week). As of early 1981, these ranged from $20 to $67. In most cases, the level is changed infrequently, despite rising wage levels which in time make it easier to meet the requirement with fewer hours of work per week. The minimum weekly earnings re-quirement should be set as a fraction of the state average weekly wage in covered work so that the amount required adjusts periodically for wage level changes. The fraction should be small, such as one-fifth or one-sixth, so as not to screen out low-wage workers, yet high enough to be meaningful. Ohio's average weekly wage in 1978 was $256; its weekly wage requirement has been $20 for many years, now well under one-twelfth of the average wage; it probably should be about $50 in 1981. Most weeks-of-work states are below the appropriate level. The high-quarter multiple requirements also tend to specify minimum high-quarter or base-period earnings requirements that are not in keeping with current average wage levels. These earnings requirements should also be related to the average wage.

There may be some reluctance to require states with very easy minimum requirements, such as a flat-earnings test, to adopt the stiffer tier 1 test since it would eliminate from eligibility marginal, usually low-paid workers who have been unable to find adequate and more steady work. The higher requirement would also screen out people who want only a little part-time work or who limit their employment to very short term seasonal activity. Under JSS, if the claimants eliminated represent cases of genuine need, are from low-income households, and are available for and actively seeking work, they would likely be eligible for unemployment assistance.

One other point needs to be made with respect to how a claimant's base-period exprience is applied to the qualifying requirements. Most states now define the claimant's base period as the first four of the last five completed calendar quarters prior to the first claim. That leaves a gap of from three to six months. (It is even more in a few states.) In most states, information about the base-period experience to be measured is contained in agency files accumulated for each covered worker from quarterly earnings reports filed by employers in conjunction with their state UI tax returns. These reports are not submitted until about a month or more after a quarter ends. More time is needed to post the data. This process accounts for the gap. Some states do not maintain worker quarterly wage records but instead request wage and employment information from former employers when a claimant files a first claim. In these states, there is no gap; the most recent months and weeks are included in the base period. Where a gap exists, as it does in most states, claimants may fail to meet the requirements simply because the most recent employment is not included in the base period. That result is more likely for a recent new entrant or reentrant to the labor force. Often, such claimants are advised to wait and refile after the turn of another quarter. In the interest of reducing the effects of such unequal approaches, it may be appropriate to require states to take account of the most recent employment, if the claimant falls short of the requirement, by requesting a report from the recent employer(s).

To sum up, the proposed qualifying requirements and the potential benefit duration for each tier are as follows:

	Tier 1	Tier 2	Tier 3
Potential duration	13 weeks	13 weeks	13 weeks
Minimum requirement:			
Base-period employment	14-20 weeks	26 weeks	39 weeks (or 52 weeks in 2-year base period)
or			
High-quarter earnings multiple equivalent	1.1-1.5	2.0	3.0 (or 4.0 in 2-year base period)

The NCUC has recommended that state minimum qualifying requirements should not be less than 14 weeks of base-period employment. It recommends the weeks-of-work form of the test or the high-quarter multiple equivalent. The Commission did not recommend a ceiling for the minimum requirement but did urge states to lower their requirements for 26 weeks of potential duration substantially below 39 weeks of work; it recommended that no state be allowed to require more than 39 weeks for 26 weeks of benefits. As noted earlier, the NCUC favored triggered extended benefit duration during periods of high unemployment for exhaustees of regular benefits.

The proposed three-tier program would operate so that the movement from one tier to the next would be a distinct, formal process that makes clear to the claimant, and also stresses to the administrative staff, that unemployment has reached a new and more serious stage requiring different attitudes toward the search for work and, perhaps, different approaches. Although the tier qualifying threshold points may be arbitrary, they nevertheless serve the purpose of signaling a fresh view of the claimant's problem and help to create a different psychological atmosphere conducive to speedier reemployment.

Continuing eligibility and disqualifications

Besides meeting minimum qualifying requirements, claimants now must satisfy other conditions to be eligible, and to remain eligible, for benefits. These conditions would continue to apply under the three-tier program. What would change, however, is the kind of benefit disqualifications imposed for failure to meet those conditions.

Under present UI laws, state disqualification provisions vary considerably. They have become generally more severe in recent years. Leaving a job voluntarily without good cause or being discharged for misconduct have always warranted a suspension of benefits. The same is true for refusing an offer of a suitable job without good cause. In the past, most states suspended benefits for a limited period of time after which the claimant could draw benefits if still unemployed and otherwise eligible. The theory was that unemployment continuing beyond the suspension period is caused by labor market conditions and is no longer the result of the claimant's own act. By now, however, the majority of states have adopted provisions calling for benefit suspensions lasting throughout the claimant's current unemployment; benefits become payable only after the claimant has worked again for at least a specified amount of time (or earned at least a specified amount) and is then laid off under qualifying circumstances. Other states still suspend benefits for a limited period, most from 4 to 13 weeks. In addition to benefit suspension, some states also reduce a disqualified claimant's potential duration entitlement.

Under the three-tier program, no state would suspend benefits for more than 13 weeks for a voluntary quit or misconduct discharge disqualification. For refusal of a suitable job, the suspension would not exceed 6 weeks while the claimant is in tier 1; it could be as long as 13 weeks after tier 1, allowing states the opportunity to increase pressure on the claimant to accept a broader range of job offers or referrals. In no case would benefit rights be reduced or canceled.

One reason for the recently increased severity of state disqualification provisions is that many employers strongly object to the payment of post-suspension benefits to a former employee who left the job or was fired for misconduct, especially when those benefits can contribute to an increase in the employer's tax rate. That is seen as "adding insult to injury." Some states have eased this issue by not charging these benefits to the individual employer's account and by pooling the costs among all employers instead. A suspension lasting as long as two or three months appears harsh enough for the disqualified claimant. The more aggressive pursuit of new employment under the proposed Job Security System and the closer review of the claimant's job search activity can help prevent malingering, which is commonly attributed to disqualified claimants and is another reason advanced for severe treatment.

The guideline long urged by the federal government for setting the length of the benefit suspension for job separation disqualifications has been the average duration of a spell of unemployment. Presumably, the average claimant should find a new job in that time; unemployment beyond that point is considered the result of poor employment conditions and not the claimant's fault. That unemployment, it is argued, has become involuntary, and the claimant should be entitled to draw benefits. Historically, the average spell duration has ranged generally from about five to eight weeks, depending on economic conditions. The average, however, may be badly understated by the inclusion of unemployment spells of workers on short term layoffs who do not seek other jobs. The average for permanently separated workers is probably higher and therefore may be a more appropriate guide for the suspension period for disqualified workers. Allowing suspensions lasting up to 13 weeks seems consistent with this line of reasoning. The more moderate suspension period for a job refusal in tier 1 reflects the less certain circumstances that surround this disqualification. The related issues of what is a "suitable" job and what constitutes good cause for refusal leave enough room for uncertainty about the accuracy of the decision as to warrant giving the claimant the benefit of the doubt in this way, especially in the early stages of unemployment.

A claimant who becomes unable to work or is not available for work is disqualified from benefits during the period involved. The same rule would apply under the three-tier program. One present exception that would continue to apply is that a claimant who undertakes approved training remains eligible to draw benefits even though not available to take a job while training. Failure, without good cause, to seek work in ways appropriate to the claimant's occupation and labor market, or in keeping with a job search plan developed with JSS staff, also would result in a disqualification.

Some state laws spell out conditions of availability for work, active search for work, and the suitability of work in specific terms. In most cases, the statutory conditions are expressed in general terms, or allow for circumstances under which the conditions may be applied differently. For example, registration for work at a local employment office generally is required, but there are exceptions. Besides registration, the law usually calls for an active or reasonable search for work by the claimant, but how active and in what manner are frequently left to the discretion of the administrative staff. Most state laws specify the criteria for "suitability" of the work the claimant should seek or accept, and there has been some tendency in recent years for these provisions to become more specific and less flexible. Most notably, several states have spelled out in their laws precise reductions in wage levels, relative to the claimant's former wage or weekly benefit amount, that the claimant would be required to accept as suitable as unemployment reaches specific duration points. Rigid application of these conditions can produce arbitrary, illogical, and unfair results in some cases. In the JSS context of periodic individualized review and counseling, well-trained staff should be capable of exercising reasonable judgment about "availability" and "suitability" so as to minimize malingering without the need for restrictively narrow statutory definitions of these terms.

The National Commission recommended less severity and less rigidity in state eligibility and disqualification provisions. It urged a limited period of benefit suspension for disqualified claimants set within a range prescribed by law and based on individual circumstances. It recommended against suspensions lasting until the claimant requalified with new employment and against reduction of a disqualified claimant's benefit rights, except in cases of fraud. With regard to provisions requiring availability and search for work and defining suitability of work, the Commission favored more general terms and their application on a case-by-case basis, taking account of relevant individual circumstances, labor market conditions, and hiring practices. The claimant's job search should be reasonable and appropriate in the light of these circumstances and judged accordingly.

The weekly benefit amount

States presently determine their own weekly benefit amount (WBA) formulas, and the variation is very wide. Except for four states which, as of January 1981, calculated the WBA as a fraction of the claimant's total base-period earnings, all formulas are designed to compensate a claimant for a fraction of the former weekly wage, usually half or more, up to a benefit maximum. The long-established objective for the WBA provision is that the great majority of claimants, or of potential claimants, should be able to receive at least half their weekly wage when unemployed.[15] Most states base the measure of the weekly wage loss on earnings in the high quarter and calculate the WBA as a fraction (usually one-twenty-sixth or more) of those earnings. Others average the weekly wage directly over the actual weeks of employment in the base period and set the WBA as a fraction, ranging from one-half to two-thirds, of that average wage. Only two states used high-quarter formulas in 1981 which resulted in WBAs of less than half the weekly wage (less than one-twenty-sixth high-quarter earnings) at levels below the maximum.

The major barrier to the achievement of the WBA objective has been the benefit ceilings in state laws. These have

---

15. This objective was first stated by President Eisenhower in the mid-1950s in an Economic Report and has been reiterated many times since by succeeding Administrations.

generally been too low in many states, relative to general wage levels, so that large proportions of claimants are unable to receive half or more of their weekly wage as intended by the basic formulas. In 1979, nationally, about 40 percent of all claimants were at the maximum WBA, meaning that most of them received less than half their wage. In 10 states, over half the claimants were at the ceiling.[16] In the four states which calculate the WBA as a fraction of annual earnings, claimants can and do receive less than half their weekly wage at all benefit levels, not only at the maximum.

Under the three-tier program, because federal UI tax revenues would be heavily involved in financing benefits, a greater degree of uniformity among state benefit provisions would be desirable. Also desirable would be some reduction of the inequities of the different rates of weekly compensation paid by states to unemployed workers who have earned the same wage. For these reasons, two federal benefit standards would apply. One would require all state formulas to assure that, at levels below the ceiling, no claimant receives a WBA of less than half the claimant's weekly wage (or less than the equivalent high-quarter fraction of one-twenty-sixth); annual wage formulas would not be acceptable. The other standard would require the states to set their ceilings as a fraction of at least two-thirds of the state average weekly covered wage. Only 13 states set their ceilings this high as of early 1981; ceilings in about a third of the states, including several of the largest states, were less than 50 percent of their average wage levels.

For many states, the required increase in the ceiling would be a drastic and very costly change to make all at once. The National Commission recommended the same standards but with a series of steps over a period of years to reach the ceil-

---

16. *Unemployment Insurance Statistics,* October-December 1979, p. 52.

ing of two-thirds of the average wage. That approach is a sensible one.

One other problem concerns states, such as Alaska and Michigan, with average wage levels well above the national average. A maximum WBA of two-thirds the state average wage would mean a ceiling estimated at close to $300 in Alaska and about $210 in Michigan for 1981, compared with their actual 1981 ceilings of $150 and $182, respectively (excluding allowances for dependents). The ceilings that the standard would require in these states seem very high in comparison with what many workers earn in much of the country, even those at the average wage levels in their states. These ceilings also would be quite costly.[17] A modified version of the proposed standard would help moderate the problem and could be regarded as consistent with the financing arrangements for the three-tier program. Since the federal share of benefit costs in tiers 2 and 3 would be paid from funds raised from a uniform federal tax that applies to a uniform taxable wage base, some limit on the application of the two-third standard to the state average wage for the benefit ceiling may be justified. The National Commission has recommended that the taxable wage base for the federal tax eventually (by 1989) equal 65 percent of the national average annual wage in covered employment. States with average weekly wages above the national average could choose to set the required benefit ceiling at the two-third standard or as a percentage of the national average weekly

---

17. Alaska has the added problem of the effects of extreme seasonal patterns on earnings. Since a large proportion of workers in that state are unable to work year-round because of very long and cold winters, their weekly earnings tend to be much higher when they do work than would normally be the case. Many workers command higher wage rates because of these conditions and many work a great deal of overtime. The state average weekly wage level, computed on the basis of an average level of employment throughout the year, therefore seriously overstates what the average normally would be, given a more usual employment pattern. Alaska calculates the WBA as a fraction of annual rather than weekly or high-quarter earnings.

wage equal to the percentage used to determine the applicable federal taxable wage base. Assuming that the national average weekly wage for 1980 was about $275, and that a taxable wage base equal to 65 percent of the 1980 national average annual wage was in force for 1981, then no state ceiling would need to be higher than $179 in that year. As of early 1981, eight states had ceilings above $179, most of them only when dependents are taken into account.

Not much attention has been given to the minimum WBA payable. State UI weekly minimums in January 1981 ranged from $5 to $43. They were under $20 in almost half the states. In most states, minimum WBAs have gone up very little or not at all over recent years despite steadily rising wage levels. Relatively few UI recipients draw the minimum or near minimum weekly amounts and little is known about them. Many probably are claimants who had worked part time. Even at the $3.35 federal minimum wage level applicable in 1981, a worker employed for only 20 hours a week can earn $67 and qualify for a $34 benefit at the 50 percent replacement rate. Only 10 states had a minimum this high as 1981 began. Minimum WBAs are clearly behind the times. While not a very important factor as far as UI is concerned, the UI minimum takes on more significance for weekly unemployment assistance amounts, as explained in chapter VI.

One approach that seems reasonable is to relate the UI minimum WBA to the minimum amount of weekly earnings specified in the qualifying requirement. The suggestion made above with respect to the qualifying requirement is to set the minimum weekly earnings required as a fraction (one-fifth or one-sixth) of the statewide average weekly covered wage. Based on estimated 1980 state average weekly wages, a minimum weekly earnings requirement of one-fifth and a 50 percent replacement rate, minimum WBAs in 1981 probably would exceed \$20 in all states (perhaps only Puerto Rico would be lower).

Dependents' allowances also affect the WBA. Thirteen states currently take account of dependents in their formulas. The standards discussed above apply to benefits before dependents are considered. Under the three-tier program, states would continue to be free to add dependents' allowances if they wish, but the proportion of the claimant's weekly wage compensated by the WBA, including allowances, would not exceed 75 percent in any case. A higher proportion, as can occur now in a few states for a claimant with many dependents, may come too close to the claimant's take-home wage level and seriously weaken the work-incentive effect of the benefit-wage differential.

Partial or reduced weekly benefits

All states have partial benefit formulas so that a claimant can draw a reduced WBA if the normal work schedule is reduced appreciably, or if the claimant takes temporary part-time work while waiting to return to a regular job or while looking for a full-time job. Most partial benefit formulas, however, given little encouragement to such part-time employment even when it is available and desirable as a temporary measure. Nor do they encourage work sharing, whereby an employer keeps all workers employed but on a temporarily reduced schedule rather than lay off completely part of the workforce. Under most formulas, the amount earned (or most of it) is offset against the WBA so that even moderate earnings tend to wipe out all benefits leaving little or no incentive to take such employment or to share work. For example, a fairly typical provision (used by about half the states) holds that a claimant earning as much as or more than the WBA can receive no benefit at all; if less is earned, the full WBA is reduced by the amount earned less a modest portion (a "disregard") ranging usually from \$2 to \$15 or from 20 to 40 percent of the WBA. In most other states, the provision is very similar except that a partial benefit is payable if the claimant's earnings come to less than the WBA plus the amount of the disregard.

Recent interest in work sharing has focused greater attention on the limitations of present partial UI benefit formulas. Work sharing is used extensively and successfully in other industrial nations with UI provisions that accommodate that approach. California has been experimenting with UI provisions which make work sharing feasible and worthwhile.[18] A temporarily reduced workweek may be a better response than total layoffs to a brief business slump. Continued work experience and fringe benefits are important considerations. If a full layoff eventually is necessary, a reduced workweek for a period before that event may help the worker find new employment while still employed. Job search prospects are almost always better for an employed worker than an unemployed one. Partial benefit provisions should help support work sharing under controlled conditions.

Where partial benefits are payable in the case of a reduced work schedule, the work reduction should be a general one applicable to all workers in a plant or establishment, or to a well-defined class of such workers. The reduction should be temporary. Other conditions may have to apply to assure that a bona fide reduction has occurred. If the reduction continues beyond a certain period of time, and other suitable full-time job opportunities are available, affected workers should be referred to such jobs.

A partial benefit formula designed to encourage a claimant to accept temporary part-time work or a reduced work schedule in place of a total layoff should allow the worker to

18. Fred Best, *Work Sharing: Issues, Policy Options and Prospects* (Kalamazoo, MI: The W.E. Upjohn Institute for Employment Research, 1981).

increase his total income (reduced earnings plus the partial benefit) above what it would be if he were totally unemployed and drawing his full WBA. The formula should not, however, result in total income equal to what the claimant earned when fully employed.

Under the three-tier program, state partial benefit formulas would provide a partial WBA to claimants who take temporary part-time jobs or have a temporary work-schedule reduction as part of a general work sharing plan. Separate formulas would apply for each type of reduced earnings. In the case of a temporary part-time job, a partial WBA would be payable if the claimant earns no more than 75 percent of his usual full-time wage or one-and-one-half times his WBA, whichever is less. The full WBA would be reduced by a fraction of not more than two-thirds of the claimant's current earnings. In the case of work sharing, a partial benefit would be payable when the reduced schedule is not more than 80 percent of the normal workweek, such as a reduction from five to four days. The partial WBA payable would be the proportion of the full WBA that the hours of work lost represented of the normal workweek. A week of partial benefits would count as a part-week against the claimant's total benefit entitlement. Thus, a partial benefit equal to half the full WBA would count as a half-week against the claimant's total entitlement.

Claimants who take temporary part-time work could receive a partial benefit at any time during any of the three tiers. Partial benefits payable under work sharing plans would be payable only in tiers 1 and 2 and for only the equivalent of 13 full weeks of benefits.

The National Commission recommended that states change their partial benefit formulas so that claimants would be encouraged to take part-time jobs. It suggested that the WBA be reduced by a percentage rather than all of the earnings made. The Commission took no position with regard to work sharing plans and their relationship to partial benefit provisions. It did urge continued research and evaluation of the various proposals and the issues involved.

One other type of partial benefit is introduced under the three-tier program, although on an experimental basis in a few states at first. It would be payable only in tier 3 to a claimant who accepts new full-time employment at wages well below wages earned in previous employment. The partial benefit would constitute a temporary wage supplement to induce a claimant who had been unemployed for 26 or more weeks to take a lower-paying job. The partial WBA would be calculated in the same way as for that payable to a claimant taking a temporary part-time job.

Cost Estimates for the Three-Tier Program

Estimates have been prepared of the size and costs of the three-tier program compared with existing UI programs. They are based on a model constructed from information obtained on the 1976 National Survey of Income and Education and from other studies of labor force experience. The model can be applied to estimate benefit costs generated by alternative state UI provisions for given years at specified rates of unemployment.[19] Through this model, U.S. Department of Labor staff has developed estimates for the three-tier program and existing programs under specified assumptions. The estimates must be regarded as tentative since there may be some question about the model's capacity to determine accurately for each state the eligibility of unemployed workers for the three tiers based on the employment and earnings information it contains. National estimates are

---

19. The model was prepared by The Urban Institute for the National Commission on Unemployment Compensation and the U.S. Department of Labor for use in estimating the costs and effects of Commission recommendations and of other possible changes in UI.

probably more reliable than the individual state estimates; the national figures are totals of the state figures.[20]

With these reservations in mind, the national estimates that were prepared for the three-tier program and the existing UI programs are presented in table 3. The following conditions and assumptions apply for the estimates:

1. The state provisions used for existing UI programs are as of January 1980.

2. January 1980 state WBA provisions apply for the three-tier estimates rather than the WBA provisions proposed above.

3. The qualifying requirements applied for each state for tier 1 eligibility are 14 weeks of base-period employment and total base-period earnings equal to 14 times 20 percent of the statewide average weekly covered wage estimated for 1979.

4. The qualifying requirement applied for tier 3 is 26 weeks of work in the base period, the same as for tier 2, rather than 39 weeks. The proposed alternative for tier 3 of 52 weeks in the base period and preceding year for those with less than 39 weeks of base-period work was not applied since the longer record is not available. The result is some overstatement of the number of tier 3 claimants and benefit costs. (Estimates of tier 3 costs when applying a 39-weeks requirement are about 7 to 10 percent less than those eligible with a 26-weeks test; the alternative requirement would reduce the differences.)

5. Three-tier estimates do not reflect proposed disqualification provisions.

---

20. Puerto Rico and the Virgin Islands are not included in these estimates.

Table 3
National Estimates of Benefit Costs and Claimants Under Existing UI Programs and the Proposed Three-Tier Program, 1980

Item	Unemployment rate assumed			
	5.5 percent	6.6 percent	7.5 percent	8.5 percent
	(dollar estimates in millions; others in thousands)			
Persons with unemployment	19,260	20,943	22,384	24,002
Persons eligible				
Regular UI benefits	8,152	9,086	9,913	10,780
Tier 1 benefits	7,962	8,877	9,690	10,542
First payments				
Regular UI program	6,625	7,629	8,548	9,318
Extended benefits	33	210	1,050	2,412
First payments				
Tier 1 benefits	6,395	7,354	8,268	9,018
Tier 2 benefits	2,489	3,066	3,700	4,179
Tier 3 benefits	1,117	1,492	1,875	2,194
Exhaustions				
Regular UI program	1,220	1,643	2,062	2,414
Extended benefits	20	127	652	1,450
Exhaustions				
Tier 1 benefits	2,620	3,253	3,901	4,418
Tier 2 benefits	1,117	1,492	1,875	2,194
Tier 3 benefits	536	765	1,009	1,137
Benefits paid				
Regular UI program	$9,186	$11,256	$13,139	$14,771
Extended benefits	29	171	1,047	2,415
Total	**$9,215**	**$11,427**	**$14,186**	**$17,186**
Benefits paid				
Tier 1 benefits	$6,350	$7,580	$8,668	$9,658
Tier 2 benefits	2,631	3,387	4,140	4,734
Tier 3 benefits	1,196	1,671	2,130	2,497
Total	**$10,177**	**$12,638**	**$14,938**	**$16,889**

SOURCE: Estimates provided by staff of Office of the Assistant Secretary for Policy Evaluation and Research, U.S. Department of Labor.

6. The estimates are for the year 1980 with the average (total) unemployment rate assumed at four different levels:

   a. 5.5 percent
   b. 6.6 percent
   c. 7.5 percent
   d. 8.5 percent

7. Estimates of extended benefits as provided under existing programs are based on the estimated triggering of EB on and off, by state and nationally, throughout the year. EB is estimated payable under each assumed unemployment rate on a calendar quarter rather than weekly basis. The national EB program is estimated to trigger on only under the assumed 8.5 percent rate, and remains on throughout the year. Under each of the other assumed rates, the number of states triggered on, by number of quarters, are as follows:

Unemployment rate	Total on	One quarter	Two quarters	Three quarters	Four quarters
5.5	3	2	0	1	0
6.6	11	8	1	0	2
7.5	27	9	11	2	5

The estimates in table 3 show that total benefits paid out by the three-tier program would exceed total outlays of the existing regular and EB programs under three of the assumed unemployment rates, and would be less only under the 8.5 percent rate. Total outlays compare as follows:

	Assumed unemployment rates			
	5.5	6.6	7.5	8.5
	(billions)			
Existing programs	$ 9.2	$11.4	$14.2	$17.2
Three-tier program	10.2	12.6	14.9	16.9

Most of the difference arises from EB outlays compared with tier 3 outlays. The latter exceed total EB payments at all assumed unemployment levels, although by only $82 million at the 8.5 percent rate. At lower assumed unemployment levels, the difference is over $1 billion in each case. It is interesting to note that regular UI program outlays total about $200 million to $300 million more than tier 1 and tier 2 benefits combined at each unemployment level. The effect, then, of the three-tier approach is some shifting of benefits to better attached and longer term unemployed workers.

The pattern indicated by these cost estimates seems clear. At lower levels of unemployment, the three-tier program would pay out more in benefits than the present system. As unemployment rises, and extended benefits become increasingly widespread, the difference narrows. At some point, outlays under the present UI system would exceed three-tier outlays.

Another observation worth noting here is that tier 1 accounts for well over half the estimated total benefit costs of the three-tier program. The range is from 57 to 62 percent—the lower the rate of unemployment, the higher the proportion. Tier 3 accounts for 12 to 15 percent of total costs, rising with increased unemployment. Considering tiers 1 and 2 only, as some approximation of the regular UI program, tier 1 costs range from 67 to 71 percent of the two tiers, indicating how much UI costs concentrate in the first 13 weeks of unemployment.

Somewhat fewer unemployed workers would qualify for tier 1 benefits than for regular benefits under January 1980 provisions. For states with flat annual earnings requirements, such as California, the 14-weeks test for tier 1 would be more restrictive. In some other states, the 14-weeks requirement would qualify more than would the current test, such as 20 weeks in New York. The base-period total earnings test applied for tier 1, however, may be stiffer than earnings required by the existing provision, thereby offsetting some of this difference. On balance, the tier 1 test appears to be more demanding overall. Under the proposed three-tier programs described above, states would be free to set the tier 1 requirement anywhere from 14 to 20 weeks. To the extent they are set closer to 20 weeks, fewer claimants would qualify for tier 1.

Under the regular UI program, the exhaustion rate rises with the level of unemployment. Based on table 3 estimates, these rates follow the expected pattern ranging from about 18 percent under the 5.5 percent unemployment rate to 26 percent under the 8.5 percent rate (table 4).[21] Comparable exhaustion rates under the three-tier system are not quite as clear-cut. Appropriate comparisons are with exhaustees of tier 2 plus tier 1 exhaustees who did not draw any tier 2 payments, presumably because they could not qualify, although a few may have returned to work at that point. Adding the two together, the exhaustees of the first two tiers represent exhaustion rates running about one percentage point more than the rates under the regular program, at all four assumed unemployment levels. Tier 1 exhaustees who did not go on to tier 2 were only about 10 percent of the total exhausting tiers 1 or 2, but enough to account for the higher rate as compared with the regular program. These claimants draw for 13 weeks but do not meet the 26-weeks work test of tier 2; many would draw additional weeks under the regular program in some states and return to work before exhausting. On the other hand, many regular benefit exhaustees who draw more than 13 but less than 26 weeks of benefits would qualify for tier 2 and be eligible for 26 weeks

---

21. Exhaustion rates as used in this analysis are lower than what they would be if they could be calculated the usual way whereby the total of exhaustees for a 12-month period is taken as a percent of first payments totaled for a 12-month period ending 6 months earlier. With the lag in the periods of the two totals—not possible with the data developed for the estimates—first payments would be lower for the lagged period than for the period of the exhaustee count (much lower as unemployment rises) and the exhaustion rates therefore would be higher.

Table 4
**Comparison of Estimated Exhaustion Rates Under Regular, EB, and
Three-Tier UI Programs, 1980**

	Exhaustion rates[1]			
	Assumed unemployment rates of:			
Program	5.5 percent	6.6 percent	7.5 percent	8.5 percent
Regular program	18.4%	21.5%	24.1%	25.6%
Tiers 1 and 2[2]	19.5	23.0	25.1	27.0
EB program	60.6	60.5	62.2	60.1
Tier 3	48.0	51.3	53.8	51.8
Regular and EB programs	18.2	20.4	19.5	15.6
Three-tier program	10.4	12.9	14.6	15.3

SOURCE: Table 3 data.

1. Estimated number of exhaustions in 1980 as a percent of first payments in 1980; these
rates understate the more accurate rates based on first payments in year ending 6 months
earlier.

2. Includes tier 1 exhaustees who did not draw tier 2 benefits.

of benefits in all. Some might, therefore, be carried long
enough so that they return to work before exhausting tier 2.
These offsetting effects seem to balance out in a way leading
to a higher exhaustion rate under tiers 1 and 2 than under the
regular program. The rates under the two programs are
close, however, possibly within the range of estimating er-
rors.

The tier 3 exhaustion rate ranges between 48 and 54 percent of those receiving tier 3 payments.[22] The EB exhaustion
rate runs about 60-62 percent at all assumed unemployment
levels. The uniform 13-week addition of tier 3 appears to
cover the need for longer protection more adequately than
does the largely variable EB addition.

22. With the 26 weeks-of-work test applied for tier 3, the assumption is that all tier 2 exhaustees go on to draw tier 3. Some actually would not because the tier 3 test (39 weeks of
work or the alternative) would screen them out, but probably not enough to make any important difference in these comparisons.

These estimates, then, indicate that, compared with regular benefits, the three-tier program would qualify somewhat fewer claimants for benefits, but a slightly higher proportion of claimants paid may exhaust their entitlement under tiers 1 and 2 than do regular UI claimants. Adding tier 3, however, reduces the total program exhaustion rate considerably, ranging from 10 to 15 percent, depending on the level of unemployment. Adding EB to the regular program in the periods payable results in final regular-EB exhaustion rates that run a good deal higher than the three-tier exhaustion rates until unemployment is high enough to trigger on EB nationally year-round. At that point, the two exhaustion rates are about the same.

VI. UNEMPLOYMENT ASSISTANCE

The proposed Job Security System includes a new unemployment assistance program as a major backstop to UI. UA would be available to unemployed workers from low-income households who do not receive UI. These include jobless workers who are not covered by UI, do not meet the UI qualifying requirements, or who have exhausted UI. UA would be a federal program financed by general revenues but administered by state job security agencies.

As proposed, the new program would replace the federally-subsidized state AFDC programs and state or local general assistance insofar as these programs now provide support to unemployed workers. Eligible UA claimants would report their employment and job search status on a weekly basis and receive payments for weeks of unemployment. They would be subject to treatment and monitoring similar to UI claimants with regard to job search assistance, counseling, and continuing eligibility.

Justification for UA

Several considerations enter into the rationale for a new federal UA program. One is the desirability of treating unemployed workers who need income support primarily as jobseekers rather than as welfare cases. For the past 20 years, welfare program amendments and reform proposals have laid increasing stress, through incentives and requirements, on moving adult recipients into labor force activity aimed at making them more or entirely self-supporting. With certain exceptions, adult recipients of AFDC must register at the employment service and be available for placement in jobs, training programs, or subsidized public employment. The WIN program is designed specifically to help move these individuals into such activity.[1] Still, their cash support continues to come from the same program supporting persons who are not required to be available for work or training, such as mothers of children under school age and those caring for sick or disabled family members. This mixture of cases that emphasize work orientation with cases that do not tends to blur the emphasis. Recent welfare reform proposals continue to lump together the work- and nonwork-oriented with respect to cash assistance. A UA program for the former would carry to a more logical footing the policy of moving capable welfare recipients from welfare to work.

Under the proposed UA program, recipients would claim their cash assistance on a weekly basis. The basis of the claim and the payment would relate to employment rather than welfare circumstances. With some frequency, recipients would receive close counseling concerning employment possibilities, job search, training, and other types of adjustments or actions to improve their vocational capabilities. They would thereby be encouraged to see themselves chiefly as jobseekers and not mainly as welfare cases, and to apply themselves accordingly. The same view of them by administrative staff would also contribute to the emphasis on work orientation.

As proposed, UA would also embrace low-income unemployed workers who are not supported by present

---

1. The WIN (Work Incentive) program has operated since 1968; for a recent account of that program's operations, see *Employment and Training Report of the President,* 1980, pp. 50-54.

welfare programs. AFDC is confined to households with dependent children and, in about half the states, to single-parent households. State and local general assistance is unevenly available or very restrictive. Various welfare reform proposals have aimed at including in AFDC all two-parent families and unemployed persons without children (childless couples and, less often, single individuals), but with no success to date.

UA, financed fully from federal funds, would relieve the states of some of the current financial burdens of welfare, another aim of reform proposals. These burdens fall unevenly on the states and reflect uneven levels of support and treatment.

Another consideration in support of UA is the need to place limits on the employer-financed UI program. The reasoning for a 39-week limitation for UI was discussed earlier. Besides the duration limit, the application of increasingly stiff qualifying requirements, tier by tier, while desirable for insurance benefits based on rights earned through employment, would screen out some marginal workers. UA would apply less stringent work qualifying requirements, and would give credit for the time spent in vocational training and education or for other evidence of labor force activity. The sentiment for maintaining low UI qualifying requirements or for extending UI benefit duration for extremely long periods is understandable when no adequate, alternative income support exists for workers with limited past employment or very long term unemployment problems who need support. Stretching UI to cover these needs weakens that program's insurance character and is more costly than confining such support to low-income cases.

Eligibility Requirements

To qualify for UA, unemployed workers would have to meet a household income test and tests of past and current labor force attachment. The present AFDC program does not apply a prior work requirement, except for unemployed fathers where states have adopted this added segment of AFDC. To be eligible for AFDC, the unemployed father in the household must have qualified for UI during the past year, or worked in at least 6 of the last 13 calendar quarters. AFDC means tests place limitations on household income and assets.[2] No prior work test applies for general assistance; a means test is the principal eligibility rule.

Income Test for UA

The measurement of "need" proposed for UA eligibility is less limiting than present welfare tests. Only income would be a factor; assets would not be considered. Moreover, UA is not intended to be limited to unemployed workers whose families have been reduced to poverty; the income test's objective aims instead at excluding those from households where income continues at a reasonable level despite the claimant's unemployment. By and large, eligible UA claimants would be from families with no other working members, or with working members who contribute relatively little to the financial support of their households. This concept for the income test would distinguish UA from the usual welfare identification with poverty; UA would occupy a middle position between welfare and UI.

The approach recommended for the income test links to the lower living standard budget developed and estimated annually by the Bureau of Labor Statistics (BLS).[3] A similar

---

2. While AFDC has no income test as such, income received is offset against the amount of the AFDC payment; the offset for wage income is restricted to two-thirds of the amount earned less a disregard of $30; other income is offset fully.

3. BLS has developed three levels of an annual urban family budget representing a "lower," "intermediate," and "higher" standard of living for a four-person family of a particular composition (a working man, his nonworking wife, and two school-age children). Each autumn, BLS prices or updates the costs of these budgets and publishes results some months later for selected metropolitan areas and the U.S. See BLS Bulletin No. 1570-05, "Three Standards of Living for an Urban Family of Four Persons" (Spring 1967), U.S. Department of Labor.

approach is taken as the basis of income eligibility for CETA services. The lower level budget represents a "below-normal" standard to which a family may be reduced because of a temporary loss of income. It is not a "minimal" or poverty-level standard.

For example, the U.S. lower level budget estimate for an urban, four-person family as of autumn 1979 was $12,585.[4] The total included $10,234 for consumption expenditures and $2,351 for income taxes, social security contributions, and other nonconsumption items. The 1979 poverty threshold for a nonfarm family of four persons was $7,412.[5] These estimates can be adjusted for different family sizes. Claimants filing for UA following the date when budget data become available would have to meet a household income test based on this lower level budget estimate. The test applied could require that the household income during the prior 12 months (or during the past 6 or 3 months and annualized) not exceed the appropriate total budget level or, if a more stringent test is desired, the total of consumption costs within that budget. The household income test should be applied periodically (after 3 or 6 months) to take account of changes in income or family size.

Some geographic or urban-rural variation may be desirable for the household income test. Since the UA weekly amount payable is wage-related, either directly or through a relationship to a UI weekly amount (see below) based on state provisions, state income tests that reflect cost-of-living

4. "Autumn 1979 Urban Family Budgets and Comparative Indexes for Selected Urban Areas," *News*, U.S. Department of Labor, Bureau of Labor Statistics, Washington, DC, April 30, 1980.

5. U.S. Bureau of the Census, Current Population Reports, Series P-60, No. 125, *Money Income and Poverty Status of Families and Persons in the United States: 1979* (Advance Report), U.S. Government Printing Office, Washington, DC, 1980.

variations among states may be appropriate. There are various possibilities for "fine-tuning" an income test.[6]

Prior work requirements

The UA claimant must also give evidence of recent labor force attachment. The objective is to make UA broader in scope than UI so that it would admit workers who are not covered by UI or not able to meet the UI qualifying requirements. The following requirements are proposed for UA to allow a wider gate, yet also to keep some reasonable basis for assuring attachment. The suggestions are tentative, since there is little experience with their adequacy for the purpose.

To qualify, the claimant must meet one of the following tests:

1. Drew UI during the last year.

2. Worked at least 14 weeks during the last year, with earnings each week equal to at least 15 percent of the statewide average weekly covered wage.[7]

3. Worked at least 10 weeks during the last year with the same minimum weekly earnings as above, and registered at least 8 weeks at the employment service (ES). As an alternative, required ES registration can be equal to 2 weeks for each week the claimant is short of the 14-weeks employment requirement.

4. Attended at least 26 weeks during the last year at a senior high school or institution of higher education,

---

6. The CETA program issues each year a set of income eligibility standards varying by family size, by county, and by metropolitan or non-metropolitan area. See "Labor Department Revises Income Levels Used for CETA Eligibility," *News*, U.S. Department of Labor, Employment and Training Administration, Washington, DC, June 2, 1980.

7. This compares with the 20 or 25 percent weekly minimum proposed earlier for the UI qualifying requirement.

or in a technical or vocational training program, provided that the education or training was completed satisfactorily.

The first requirement, of course, admits UI exhaustees from any tier. The second admits claimants who fail to meet the more stringent UI requirements. It also qualifies workers whose employment is not now covered by UI, mainly workers with employment on small farms or in domestic household service.

The third requirement is an attempt to bring in claimants with even less prior employment than 14 weeks but with the work shortfall made up by ES registration. Other alternatives could be designed involving even fewer weeks of work or more weeks of registration. Some current state UI requirements, especially when based on flat annual earnings, do admit workers to UI with less than 14 weeks of work. Having UA available for at least some of these where low income is a problem would ease the impact of stiffening the UI requirement.

The fourth requirement aims at new entrants and reentrants, particularly young people. Here, too, alternative designs could vary the number of weeks required or add a period of ES registration after school completion. The requirement for satisfactory completion of school or training is intended to induce students and trainees to stay with their work and not drop out. Many youngsters do work on jobs while in school, either part time or during summer or holiday periods. They may be able to meet the second or third requirements, or even qualify for UI, without completing school.

Persons who have not worked before, or have not worked for a year or more, and have not had schooling or training recently, would not be eligible for UA. This category may include some of the current adult recipients of AFDC. Many welfare mothers do have some employment, perhaps sporadic or unstable in nature, but sometimes enough to meet the second or third requirement. Lacking that, those who want employment or are required to be available for work in order to receive cash support should be steered into training or helped to obtain some kind of work to establish at least a foothold in the labor force.

Other requirements and disqualifications

UA recipients would have to be able to work, to be available for work, and to actively seek work. They would have to be available for full-time employment. Some recipients may have problems regarding reliable child care; such problems would be good cause for temporary nonavailability and would not be reasons for suspending UA. Claimants would be excused from the availability and job search requirements while in approved training.

Disqualifications for UA would be for the same reasons that apply for UI. UA payments would be suspended 13 weeks for voluntary leaving of work or training without good cause and for misconduct discharges. Refusal of a suitable job or training opportunity also would result in a 13-week suspension. As with UI, what constitutes "suitable" work or training would be determined on an individual basis, taking account of the claimant's prior work experience, training, education, and capabilities, as well as the duration of unemployment and current labor market conditions. In general, UA claimants could be required to reduce their job-level and wage expectations more and sooner than UI recipients.

Benefit reviewers and job search counselors would meet periodically with UA claimants to encourage and guide their job search, to consider training possibilities or other types of vocational adjustments, and to assure that claimants are available and seeking work. If some nonwork-connected problem arises that interferes with the job search or training, the UA claimant would be referred to an appropriate service or agency for assistance. No UA benefit suspension would be imposed for interruption of availability, training, or job search under such circumstances if there is good cause for the interruption, if the claimant is taking reasonable steps to overcome the problem, and if the interruption does not last beyond a limited period of time, such as four weeks or less, depending on the nature of the problem. Temporary illness or disability would not cause UA suspension if not expected to last more than a few weeks; if longer, the claimant should file for Supplementary Security Income administered by the Social Security Administration for disabled needy persons.

UA claimants waiting to qualify through a combination of work and employment service registration must be available for work and seeking work during the registration period. They should be required to report at least once during this time to consult with a UA reviewer and a jobsearch counselor concerning their activity and status. Failure to report, without good cause, would result in the loss of credit for weeks registered up to that point.

Weekly Amount of UA

As with UI, the weekly UA amount payable would be related to the claimant's recent prior earnings, if such earnings experience exists. This approach is another means of focusing on the recipient as a worker rather than as a welfare case. Although UA would be a federal program, the UA amounts payable would be set to reflect interstate variations in wages as well. The recommended approach is to have the weekly UA amounts relate to the UI WBAs.

For eligible claimants who have exhausted UI, the proposal is to set the UA weekly amount equal to 90 percent of the UI benefit. For claimants who have not received UI but qualify for UA with at least 14 weeks of work, the weekly amount would equal 90 percent of what the UI WBA would have been if based on earnings in that employment. The UA amount is set 10 percent lower than the UI level to increase incentives to take lower paying jobs.

The main problem in assigning UA amounts would arise for claimants with very little or no recent employment. These include new entrants and reentrants to the labor market, and marginal or very irregular workers. Youngsters who have recently completed their schooling and AFDC mothers are prominent among them. Many of these individuals may have worked to some extent, part time or for brief periods, while in school or when child-care arrangements could be made. Those with at least 10 weeks of employment in the past year would qualify for UA after having registered at the ES for a required period. The UA amount could be based on average earnings during the weeks worked. It would be wise, however, to consider whether or not that average is a distorted representation of the claimant's normal earning capacity. Concentrated work in short periods involving much overtime can lead to an unrepresentative weekly average. The same is true where the employment consisted of very limited part-time work. One approach would be to calculate a weekly earning capacity based on the hourly rate earned, excluding overtime, multiplied by a specified number of hours per week.

For those with no recent employment, or less than 10 weeks of work, but who qualify on the basis of completed education or training, the problem is more difficult. If it is clear that the training or education could qualify the individual for a particular type of job, then the locally prevailing entry wage for that job could be used as the basis for the UA amount. If not, the federal or state statutory minimum hourly wage could be used to develop a weekly wage base for the UA amount.

The most difficult problem comes with the individual who currently receives AFDC. AFDC recipients who have had some employment during the past year would be able to qualify for UA, or might even qualify for UI. The weekly UA (or UI) amount payable, however, may be less than the cash support (prorated weekly) provided by AFDC. The AFDC amount is not related to wage experience but is, instead, more closely related to a minimal living standard concept, or some proportion of a minimal level, taking account of the number of dependent children, housing circumstances, etc. AFDC amounts provided by the states vary widely. In May 1980, for example, the average monthly AFDC payment per family ranged among the states from $87 to $384. The U.S. average payment was $271.[8] The AFDC payment thus could and often would exceed the income provided by UA or UI, especially for larger families. AFDC recipients who qualify for UI currently may choose whichever program they wish to use; they are not likely to choose the one yielding a lower level of support. Even when UI exceeds the AFDC cash support level, recipients may still prefer AFDC since it entitles them to Medicaid and housing supplements not available to UI claimants. If the UA amount is substantially less than AFDC, it would be hard to justify a policy that abruptly eliminates AFDC for persons who can work and could qualify for UA.

There appears to be no easy solution to this dilemma. One possibility is a gradual phaseout of AFDC for such persons. Over a period of time, the AFDC support they are paid could be reduced by small amounts until UA (or UI) becomes more attractive. Recent reform proposals did call for a lower cash

---

8. *Public Assistance Payments, May 1980,* U.S. Department of Health and Human Services, Social Security Administration, December 1980, p. 10.

support level for families containing adults required to be available for work. Another possibility is to add dependent children's allowances to the basic UA amount, but in states which do not add allowances to UI, the UA-UI relationship would become distorted. Another would be to allow families on AFDC to continue to receive the children's portion as a supplement to UA (or UI) to the extent needed to make up the difference. Eligibility for Medicaid and housing subsidies could also continue. Some transition approach can be devised with some protection against a sudden severe decline in the level of support in individual cases.

Although UA recipients must be available for full-time work, a partial UA amount would be provided when the claimant takes a part-time job as a temporary expedient and earns an amount per week equal to less than about 1.6 times the weekly UA amount. The full UA amount would be reduced by two-thirds of the amount earned, less a disregard of 15 percent of earnings.

UA Duration

As long as the UA recipient actively seeks work and meets all other requirements with respect to job search and counseling advice, UA would continue to be payable. No specific limit is set on its duration. Except for periods of severe and prolonged recession, it is difficult to conceive of a UA recipient being unable to obtain some kind of employment for at least 14 weeks in a year's time. Continued failure, however, to find employment or to benefit from training or some other remedial assistance would have to be construed as evidence that the recipient is not employable. After a year, unless some special circumstances justify continued UA in such cases, the recipient could be judged no longer eligible. Application for SSI as a disabled individual might be indicated.

Administration of UA

Although UA is designed as a federal program financed by federal general revenues, the states would administer UA as part of the proposed Job Security System. Its close resemblance to UI and the important application of employment services and job search assistance make the state agency the logical selection for UA administration. A separate operation would defeat the objective of treating UA claimants primarily as jobseekers.

Some UI administrators may seriously object to state agency acceptance of responsibility for UA. They may feel it would weaken or dilute efforts to maintain a high-quality UI operation. Other special programs of cash support for unemployed workers have been assigned to them over the years, often with inadequate administrative resources. That is a legitimate cause for resistance to added responsibilities. Without sufficient and well-trained staff and satisfactory support in general, UA cannot expect to achieve its objectives.

Another objection concerns the mix of the insurance and welfare concepts within the same overall administrative system. The application of an income test for UA carries the possible connotation of "inferior" status vis a vis UI. The fear is that the stigma may "rub off" on UI and that both administrative staff and the public may degrade their treatment and view of UI claimants and weaken the social insurance traditions that have helped maintain the dignity of the UI program. This, too, is a legitimate concern. The response is that, compared with the existing welfare approach for employable persons, the proposed UA program goes far to escape welfare connotations. The income test is not poverty oriented, and there is no investigation of household assets. As it is with UI, the emphasis is on employment, not need. If handled properly, there need not be any loss of status or dignity by UI claimants, and UA recipients can achieve a more favorable position than is the case when dependent on AFDC or general assistance. Much would depend on how aggressively and successfully the agency presses the objective of employment equally for both UI and UA.

Potential Cost and Impact of UA

No estimates for UA costs are available. Certainly, UA would add a new dimension and a new set of costs. To some extent, offsetting cost savings would be realized, as UA would replace other forms of support in many instances. The tendency to extend UI duration during recession through federal supplemental benefits has become well established. With UA, such extension may be less likely to occur. Because of the income test and lower weekly amount for UA, less would be paid out in UA to exhaustees than in supplemental UI benefits for the period FSB would be payable. A study of exhaustees of regular UI and EB who drew FSB in 1975-1977 found that about 30 percent were from households with money income equal to at least twice the official poverty level; the household incomes of another 14 percent were between 1.5 and 2.0 times the poverty level.[9] Assuming application of the proposed UA income test, this finding implies that almost 45 percent of all UI exhaustees under the three-tier program potentially eligible for FSB during recession periods would not qualify for UA.[10]

Where AFDC and General Assistance recipients shift to UA, offsetting cost savings would occur. For the same in-

---

9. Walter Corson and Walter Nicholson, *The Federal Supplemental Benefits Program—An Appraisal of Emergency Extended Unemployment Insurance Benefits* (Kalamazoo, MI: The W.E. Upjohn Institute for Employment Research, forthcoming 1981).

10. Using 1979 figures cited earlier for four-person families, the lower level budget was about 1.7 times the poverty threshold.

dividuals, however, it is difficult to tell if the net effect overall would be higher or lower costs.

UA would go to other workers who are not now supported by existing programs. Besides UI exhaustees who meet the income test, unemployed workers unable to qualify for UI because of limited employment might be able to qualify for UA. To the extent that states raise their UI qualifying requirements because of UA, there would be offsetting cost savings in UI. Jobseekers, especially youths, who qualify for UA on the basis of completed education or training would add a new element of cost.

Because UA is not strictly limited in duration, there may be concern about the potential costliness of such a more or less open-ended program. Moreover, the indefinite availability of UA may lower incentives to seek and take jobs. There is, of course, no duration limit on the current AFDC programs either. With an aggressive pursuit of job search and vocational adjustment, pressed by JSS staff, the expectation is that continued dependence on UA would not be indefinite. Those efforts would also help offset disincentive effects of UA, as would the lower rate of wage-loss compensation as compared with UI rates. In some cases, UA recipients who fail to find employment may be judged unemployable and removed from the UA program. They may qualify for cash support under the Supplemental Security Income program for aged and disabled persons who are unable to work.

Estimates of UA costs require data describing potential recipients by household size and income, work and earnings experience, and education or training experience. For some groups, part but not all of the information may be available by which to estimate who could qualify for UA. Eligibility of UI exhaustees and current AFDC recipients may be easiest to estimate, although the principal difficulty would be lack of household income information for UI exhaustees and work experience information for AFDC recipients. For other potential clients, the data available is even less solid. Apart from eligibility, estimates of claimant duration of UA are also quite problematical because of the lack of information about very long term unemployment experienced by low-income households as well as the potential effects of aggressive, assisted job search efforts. Some claimants, no doubt, would move in and out of employment and float between UA and UI, a difficult pattern to estimate.

While some estimates of UA costs can be made and should be pursued, their reliability may be limited or uncertain. One way to overcome the problem is to establish UA on an experimental basis in a state or two, or in a few areas, and gain some experience. Another is to begin UA slowly by making it available to one or two categories of potential recipients at first and expanding its coverage gradually. UI exhaustees, for example, may be the first candidates for UA, followed by workers not covered by AFDC, and then AFDC recipients. This order would place first emphasis on unemployed workers who have no other source of cash support.

VII. SUMMARY AND CONCLUSIONS

Summary

Reemployment is the primary objective of the proposed Job Security System. Its various programs are all designed to support that goal. Workers who lose their jobs or experience temporary layoff could turn to the JSS for job search assistance, other reemployment services, and partial wage-loss replacement through unemployment insurance or unemployment assistance. Under normal labor market conditions, most of the unemployed would return to work in a relatively short period, usually within two or three months.

When jobless workers initially file for benefits or apply for employment services, the system's first procedure would be to identify those who may face difficulty in regaining employment. The system would continue to work with claimants or applicants so identified through diagnosis of their problems, through periodic counseling to guide their job search, and by arranging for retraining or other kinds of adjustments that may enhance their employability. The Employment Service component of the JSS would have the principal responsibility for these functions but would work closely with UI and UA staff in servicing individual workers drawing income support. Matching jobseekers and job openings in good volume and across a broad range of occupations would strengthen the labor exchange function of the ES and the assistance it can provide to the unemployed and to employers in local labor markets. The ES would also be the center for labor market information. The better its detailed knowledge of current local employment conditions and the better its methods to make that knowledge directly useful to jobseekers and employers, the better its contribution to reduced unemployment and the effective use of labor resources.

Although existing state Employment Services (or Job Services) perform all of these functions to one degree or another, most are not doing so comprehensively or systematically, particularly with regard to workers with established labor force attachment—the experienced unemployed. Restriction of administrative resources over the last 15 years has limited ES capacity to serve adequately a greatly expanded labor force. ES activities have been increasingly diverted from mainstream goals to service special programs, such as registering welfare and food stamp recipients for work test purposes but with little or no genuine follow through, operating the employment and training aspects of the WIN program for adult AFDC recipients, and dealing with a variety of needs of the CETA programs. Funds allocated to cover the added costs of these activities have not been adequate. As a result, the ES has played a diminishing role in helping experienced unemployed workers regain employment. Past efforts to disassociate the ES from the UI program to improve the former's image and stature as a manpower agency only added further to that result. The proposed JSS calls for a reorientation of the ES to reemphasize the job search needs of experienced workers and a strengthening of its capacity to serve those needs.

Under the proposed system, the UI program would be restructured to support more strongly the reemployment goal. States would still specify the statutory details of UI and continue to administer the program. The federal role, however, would be expanded through the application of additional minimum standards or requirements and through increased federal financing of benefits. The new program's scope of protection would not extend beyond 39 weeks of benefits in a single year. UI would be organized into 3 successive tiers, each providing 13 weeks of benefits. In succession, the three tiers would provide compensation for short, medium, and long term unemployment. Including the long term tier, all tiers would be available at all times, without regard to variations in the level of unemployment. Claimants would have to meet increasingly stiff tests of past work attachment as they move from one tier to the next. The tests would require at least 14 to 20 weeks of work in the past year to qualify for tier 1 benefits, 26 weeks of work for tier 2, and 39 weeks of work (or 52 weeks during the last 2 years) to qualify for tier 3. The requirements governing the claimant's current availability for work and job search would also grow stricter as unemployment lengthens. UI claimants would be pressed to consider a broader range of job alternatives and lower wage levels as they move from tier to tier. Local labor market conditions would affect the intensity of the job search efforts expected of claimants. The distinct and formal procedure of moving from one tier to the next would not only emphasize the stiffer requirements, it would also require a reassessment of reemployment prospects and job search strategy. The process is meant to impress upon the claimant and staff the need for a more urgent attitude about the problem and for a willingness to consider other, perhaps less attractive, steps to regain employment. Failure by the claimant to respond reasonably to advice offered could lead to benefit suspension.

States would finance all benefit costs of tier 1 through their own experience-rated UI taxes. State and federal UI tax revenues would finance equally the benefit costs of tier 2, while tier 3 costs would be covered entirely by federal UI taxes. This arrangement views the UI costs of short term unemployment as the responsibility of individual employers and appropriately allocates costs to them through experience-rated taxes. Individual employer responsibility for UI costs becomes less supportable as unemployment lengthens. The general condition of the labor market, changes in national and international consumer markets, foreign competition, federal policies, and other factors that exert their influence without regard to state lines are deemed more likely to account for longer term unemployment than factors that operate within states or that individual employers can control. More pooling, among employers and on a national basis, of the UI costs of longer term unemployment is therefore considered justifiable and a reasonable rationale for the new financing arrangements. These arrangements would also ease the solvency problems of state UI funds. Federal financing of longer term benefit costs, in effect, reinsures the state funds against very high and unpredictable recession costs without establishing a special reinsurance scheme for the purpose.

Under the proposed program, federal minimum standards would apply to state weekly benefit amount provisions to reduce the present uneven treatment around the country of UI claimants with the same wage experience. The standards would require compensation of at least half the claimant's weekly wage loss up to a maximum amount that is not less than two-thirds of the statewide average weekly wage in covered employment. Revised partial benefit provisions would offer more incentives than do present provisions for claimants to take temporary part-time work. They would encourage and accommodate work sharing as an alternative to full layoffs.

Estimates indicate that the total benefit costs of the three-tier UI program would exceed the costs of the current program of regular and extended benefits, especially when unemployment rates are low. The difference would diminish as these rates increase and disappear at high rates of unemployment. Estimates also show that tier 1 costs would account for about 60 percent of all benefits under the three tiers.

With a 39-week limit, the UI program's integrity as a social insurance program would be better preserved than has been the case during the recessions of the 1970s when supplemental benefits extended the length of UI protection beyond that limit. To meet the needs of UI exhaustees and of other unemployed workers not eligible for UI, the JSS would provide a new program of Unemployment Assistance. UA would be payable to unemployed workers who meet both a past employment test and a household income test. The former test would be less stringent than that for UI eligibility and allow for some substitution of registered job search time or time spent in training for weeks of employment. The suggested income test would apply an eligibility threshold equivalent to the lower level living standard budget estimated annually by the Bureau of Labor Statistics. This level is well above the official poverty line but still likely to exclude about 45 percent of UI exhaustees from UA eligibility. UA weekly cash benefits would be wage-related, but lower than UI benefits.

UA recipients would be subject to the same job search and counseling review procedures as UI claimants. They would, however, be confronted with greater pressure to consider or accept a broader range of employment than that reflective of prior experience and wage levels. Current recipients of AFDC, food stamps, and general assistance who are required to be available for work would apply for UA instead. The remaining welfare programs would then be confined to nonparticipants in the labor force. With the new program, employable individuals now on welfare would be treated essentially as jobseekers and not as welfare cases. The emphasis would be on job search, week by week, rather than on the monthly or semi-monthly welfare check which is needs-related, not wage-related. Low-income unemployed workers not now eligible for UI or welfare could also apply for UA. The new program would be administered for the federal government by state JSS agencies, with all costs financed by federal general revenues.

Concluding Observations

The proposed Job Security System represents a substantial departure from existing arrangements, but it also represents a return to some of the earlier thinking about how to deal with the unemployment of workers. A major concern about unemployment insurance at the outset was with the "moral hazard" involved—the fear that UI recipients would tend to malinger, to delay returning to work. One important safeguard against this risk was a public employment service with a good labor exchange operation. Indeed, a public ES was generally regarded as a prerequisite to the establishment of UI. It was natural that UI and ES were closely linked at the beginning. The more recent weakened connection between the two may be partly responsible for the revived public concern about the disincentive effects of UI.[1] The JSS would restore the strong link. Besides applying the work test, the ES would be called upon to expand and intensify positive approaches to assist the job search of the insured unemployed. All components of the JSS are designed with the central focus on reemployment in mind. At the same time, the restructuring of UI for this purpose also aims at resolving or easing some of the problems that currently face the program. Similarly, the proposed new UA program, in

---

1. Recent studies of disincentive effects ignore or discount any offsetting effects of ES applications of the work test to claimants.

its orientation to labor force participation, seeks to solve some of the dilemmas encountered by welfare reform efforts. If it is agreed that reemployment is the appropriate central objective of public programs for the unemployed and that some of the difficulties of these programs can be diminished in the process of reorganizing them around that objective, then the JSS approach has much to recommend it.

A major question, however, is whether a strengthened and revitalized Employment Service with expanded job search assistance efforts for experienced unemployed workers can produce significant reemployment results and be cost effective. The added administrative costs will be substantial. Staff required to apply the more intensive and individualized treatments will have to be larger and more highly trained. The direct payoff is in shorter unemployment and reduced outlays for income support. Indirect benefits include more productive use of labor resources, increased wage earnings with multiplier effects on demand, greater tax revenues, more economic activity in general, and various social gains from less unemployment. Several limited experiments with more concentrated services to UI claimants, made about 10 or more years ago, offered some promise that favorable results can be achieved if such efforts are not inhibited by very poor labor market conditions.[2]

This monograph has presented the JSS proposal with a considerable amount of specific detail. The purpose is to make more tangible the ideas underlying the system and the means for their implementation. Details, of course, can vary; those suggested do not in themselves constitute a rigid set of specifications. The broader design features are more important to the system as a whole. For example, a strengthened ES refocused to promote the job search and reemployment of the experienced unemployed is crucial to

---

2. See footnote 5, ch. IV.

the scheme. Exactly how the services are organized and staffed can involve a range of alternatives. The three-tier design for the UI program is important to its support of the reemployment objective and to its phased cooperative effort with the ES as the unemployment of claimants lengthens. The details of federal rquirements and of financing patterns need not be identical to those described here, but something along the lines indicated would help ease the current issues concerning UI duration limits, benefit inequities and inadequacies among state provisions, and state UI fund insolvency. A new UA program is important to preserve the social insurance integrity of UI and at the same time meet the needs of long term unemployed workers from low-income households who are beyond the duration limits of UI protection. The extent to which UA should be available to other jobseekers, including those now receiving welfare, is a less vital question to the total JSS scheme. A broader scope for UA, however, offers a means of rationalizing the treatment of work-oriented welfare recipients and other low-income unemployed. The specific UA eligibility tests and weekly benefit levels described here are mainly illustrative.

The JSS proposal need not and probably should not be implemented all at once. It can serve as a broad plan to be achieved through a series of steps following a sequence leading eventually to the total system. A good place to start is with the employment services. Their strengthening and systematic application to UI claimants at appropriate stages of unemployment is the most important aspect of the new system to develop quickly. It will take time to perfect the approaches that work best and to shape a staff that can employ them well. Building on the U.S. Department of Labor's current Eligibility Review Program may be the way to proceed, concentrating first in a few states and then expanding to others after refinements are made. An experimental UA program could come next, perhaps confined at first to UI exhaustees, then including low-income unemployed not now eligible for welfare, and finally adding current welfare recipients who are employable. Redesign of UI may be the most difficult step to take because it involves considerable reform of existing state programs, and requires state as well as federal legislation. Federal provision of long term (tier 3) benefits at all times, applying the additional requirements and full federal financing, could be offered first as a replacement for the existing triggered EB program. Reassessment of the prospects and job search needs of claimants before they draw more than 13 weeks of benefits could also be emphasized, along with increased intensity of counseling and review services. The most significant results of the step-by-step process may be the improvements gained in diagnosing reemployment problems and in learning how best to tailor services to individual needs. Patterns that emerge in dealing with the unemployed with respect to the stages and duration of their unemployment are likely to suggest the value and best design for a tiered UI program.

The proposed system provides some new ways to think about dealing with the problems of unemployment and welfare. As existing programs age and grow subject to various degrees of rigidity, the need for fresh viewpoints increases. This monograph will serve an important purpose if it stimulates thinking and debate about these problems along new lines.